DATE DUE

S0-ARX-592

VICTORIAN PORTRAITS

Frontispiece]

HIS ROYAL HIGHNESS PRINCE ALBERT
(CONSORT OF HER MAJESTY)

"I humbly implore that the divine blessing may prosper this union and render it conducive to the interests of my people."

Vide Her Majesty's Speech, Jan. 16th, 1840

VICTORIAN PORTRAITS

By Percy Colson

Essay Index Reprint Series

BOOKS FOR LIBRARIES PRESS

FREEPORT, NEW YORK

First Published 1932
Reprinted 1968

LIBRARY OF CONGRESS CATALOG CARD NUMBER:

68-16921

PRINTED IN THE UNITED STATES OF AMERICA

DA
562
C7
1968

Ha 284968

Sr

TO

LADY STRACEY

AND

EDWARD HUTTON

LIST OF PLATES

CONTENTS

～

THE UNHAPPY PRINCE AND BARON STOCKMAR

VICTORIAN PORTRAITS

CHAPTER ONE

" 'Tis as easy as lying; govern these ventages with your
finger and thumb, give it breath with your mouth and it will
discourse most excellent music."

"Well said, old Mole! Cans't work i' the earth so fast?"

SHAKESPEARE (*Hamlet*)

WHEN in 1837 Queen Victoria came to the throne
vowing that she would "be good", England was still
struggling with the after-effects of its twenty-five years'
conflict with France, which had left it in the poverty-stricken
condition in which great wars are apt to plunge both victors
and vanquished. Revolutionary ideas and Royalty in the
person of George the Fourth and his blackguardly brothers
had alienated all respect from the throne. George's
successor—that preposterous old person, King William,
who, to do him justice, had asked nothing better than to
be left in peace with his mistress and their bastard children
—had done little to raise it in popular estimation. The
whole country was seething with discontent, and anything
might have happened. But it was neither hypocritical nor
smug. Coarse, perhaps, but none the worse for that; it
could laugh and be gay; and, curiously enough, the
succession of German Monarchs since the reign of James II
had not Germanized it.

When in 1901 Queen Victoria died, having given the

13

throne a prestige it had not enjoyed since the days of Elizabeth, she left England powerful, feared, and wealthy, and, except, perhaps, for the very rich, the dullest country in Europe in which to live. She left an England ridden by the fetish of a dreary respectability to which both Church and State bowed down and worshipped. An England in which the most natural functions of the body were considered improper and not to be mentioned, and where vice, though it flourished exceedingly, was politely ignored and driven underground. An England in which men and women had disappeared and given place to "ladies and gentlemen". And this powerful wealthy ugly civilization, built gradually up during the long reign of the Great Queen, survived her death less than fourteen years, crashing to the ground with the rest of Europe in August, 1914. Would the crash have occurred had Victoria not taken Albert the Good to the Royal Bed? It is an interesting speculation. . . .

Victoria came of age legally on her eighteenth birthday —to the great content of King William, who cordially detested his sister-in-law, the Duchess of Kent. The poor woman's position was by no means an easy one. Why had not the old King been gathered to his fathers before the majority of the young Princess, leaving her—the Duchess—to play the comfortable and profitable *rôle* of Regent, aided by her secretary, major-domo, general factotum, and *cher ami*—*"trop cher"*, they said—Sir John Conroy? Conroy was no more popular at Court than she

was. "A ridiculous fellow, a compound of the Great Hussy
and the chamberlain of the Princess of Navarre," Greville
calls him.

She had unbounded faith in him and with true Coburg
arrogance resented any attempt to snub *his*, or curtail her
own, very considerable pretensions, making herself as
unpleasant as she possibly could to King William and his
unfortunate Queen, Adelaide—a kindly harmless woman.
Stockmar in his diary describes the Duchess as "a little
animated woman, talks immensely and laughs still more.
No beauty; mouth and teeth bad. She disfigures herself still
more by distorting her mouth and blinking her eyes."

But she had her brother Leopold to fall back upon. The
Coburgs were quick to rally to the support of one another,
and he had been on the most intimate footing at Kensington
Palace during the childhood of little Victoria. In 1817 he
had married Princess Charlotte, daughter of George IV,
who lived for only a year after the marriage. He had very
prudently fallen in love with her when he came to England
in the suite of Alexander of Russia, and, after her unhappy
entanglement with the Prince of Orange, the Prince Regent
was glad enough to marry her to this respectable scion of
the Coburgs. She had had a wretched childhood; how
could it have been otherwise at that disreputable Court?
"My mother was bad," she wrote, "but she would not have
been as bad if my father had not been infinitely worse."
The alliance was an excellent one for Leopold—and for his
family. With it started the amazing luck of the Coburgs.
After her death he lived quietly at Claremont, near Esher

—which, with £50,000 a year, had been settled on him—
and occupied himself with giving advice to everyone who
would listen to him; a family speciality, this. It was usually
excellent advice, especially where the Coburg interests were
concerned, and he continued to shower it on his sister in
lengthy folios after he became King of the Belgians in 1831
and, later, on Victoria, until, on the suggestion of Lord
Melbourne, she gently hinted that she preferred to manage
her own affairs.

Leopold's Household at Claremont included a young
German doctor, Christian Friedrich Stockmar, who was
destined to wield secretly so commanding an influence in
English politics that it is not too much to say that for many
years he virtually ruled England through Prince Albert. He
was born at Coburg in 1787, his father being a prosperous
country lawyer. His family had already played some part
in the petty politics of the reigning House and had earned
its fullest confidence. "If," said one of the Dukes, "I can
lay my head on the lap of a Stockmar, I shall be safe."
Young Christian was, even as a boy, supremely sure of his
future. Once at dinner, looking at the comfortable but
modest service, he remarked, to the amusement of his
family, "Some day I must have all this of silver." He could
have had it of gold had he chosen to profit financially by
the position to which he subsequently rose. For five years
he studied medicine, which undoubtedly helped him to
acquire the extraordinary power he developed of penetrating
into the minds of people and analysing motives. One of his

first activities after he had begun to practise was to organize a war hospital at Coburg during the war years 1812-1815. (He was, by the way, one of the first to recognize the value of cleanliness and fresh air in hospitals.) It was during this period that he met Leopold, who, on his marriage, offered him the post of physician to his household.

A strange character, this young doctor. Inordinately ambitious—but with the ambition that has no wish for public applause, infinitely preferring to remain in the background and pull the strings that make the puppets dance. Intensely German and genuinely patriotic; thorough, painstaking, cold, critical and sceptical. Gifted, too, with a memory and power of observation possessed by few. His physique was weak; so was his eyesight; and before he was thirty he developed dyspepsia, which ruined his hitherto cheerful disposition and turned him into a hypochondriac. He was, like the average middle-class German, rough and unpolished, and his table manners were appalling. Like most Germans, he worshipped rank; especially princely rank. He married in 1821 and founded a family in Coburg, but for the next forty years he was too busy helping to rule England to be able to devote much time to it. Years sometimes passed without his seeing his wife or child, which, as his son tells us, "must have been a great sacrifice for so warm-hearted a man"! But if Frau Stockmar was not favoured with much of his society—and who shall say that her state was the less gracious?—she had at any rate the consolation of knowing that his conduct was pleasing to the Almighty. He never lost his "German characteristic of shaping his actions according to the highest motives".

At Claremont Stockmar soon made himself useful. There were things that paid better than medicine, he discovered, so medicine went by the board. Leopold, himself no fool, at once realized what a tactful and discreet servant he possessed, and he entrusted him with a considerable share in the complicated negotiations which established him on the Belgian throne, thereby depriving poor little Victoria of her "dearest Uncle". "Dearest Uncle", however, was neither loved nor appreciated outside Kensington Palace. Creevey writes: "Sefton went down to the House to hear the Royal messages which it was known were coming—one to enable someone to sign poor 'Prinney's' name for him, and the other to show up Leopold for having jibbed at last as to taking Greece upon himself." Later on we read: "I left Fitz-Clarence at Gosforth, and continue to like him as well as ever. He said the King was getting very old and cross and that 'Prince Leopold was a damned humbug'." Greville writes with regard to the Belgian affair: "Matuscewitz (the Russian Ambassador) told me that he went on his knees to Palmerston to send someone with him (Leopold) who would prevent his getting into scrapes," and both Talleyrand and Falck predicted disaster. Palmerston did not see his way to interfere, so Leopold "was suffered to go alone and plunge all his weakness, vanity and incapacity into the middle of their (the Belgians') turbulence, arrogance and folly". Greville was wrong: he had Stockmar with him, who knew that the new king was everywhere regarded as a disturber of the precarious tranquillity of Europe and saw to it that he made no mistakes. Stockmar did not share Greville's unfavourable opinion of his Royal patron. "Prince Leopold," he wrote, "is a complete English Gentleman: our hope in these dangerous times"! In 1835 Leopold employed him to engineer the marriage of Prince Ferdinand of Coburg to Donna Maria of Portugal—the third Coburg *coup*—and his services were rewarded with the title of Baron. Let us leave Leopold seated on the throne of his "vulgar little kingdom" and return to Coburg—that nursery of eligible princelets—whose star was beginning to shine with such disconcerting lustre.

While Victoria was growing up in England, her two cousins, Ernest and Albert, were busily engaged in the same interesting occupation at Coburg. They were the sons of the reigning Duke, whose sister had married, as her second husband, the Duke of Kent. The history of their boyhood and education has been told often enough. The "old old story" can become tedious if told too often, but in Albert's case the child was so essentially "father to the man" that it is necessary to touch briefly on its leading features.

The Duke of Saxe-Coburg was, perhaps, as poor (and as petty) a potentate as could very well be found. Napoleon's armies had taken Coburg in their stride and had dealt with it faithfully, leaving it little but its eyes—"to weep with". The Duke was not a particularly agreeable person; his character was an engaging combination of moral laxity and lofty sentiment. He ran his household with real

Teutonic precision, and the boys were brought up with Spartan rigour. "I remember," says Ernest, "that we had in a hard winter to ride across the mountains between Coburg and Gotha and to endure the most frightful cold. Thus did my father teach us the self-command of adults." They were educated with the same relentless severity. One week of Albert's daily time-table of work would cause Eton to go on strike.

No wonder that their mother, the Duchess—a charming pleasure-loving woman—considered that what was sauce for the goose was sauce for the gander, too, and sought consolation elsewhere. To be made love to by time-table—or neglected altogether—was not to be born. There were incessant scenes and various rumours—one of them, Strachey tells us, concerning an attractive Court official of Jewish extraction. Be that as it may, they were first separated and then divorced. The Duchess went to Paris, where she died in 1831. She never saw her children after the separation.

The two boys were happy enough in spite of the severe discipline and hard work—boys have a delightful faculty of extracting happiness out of anything. Albert, too, earned his title "the Good" very early. He was cheerful, docile and industrious; a bit of a prig perhaps. His brother wrote: "A decidedly *doctrinaire* manner of treating everything was peculiar to him even at an earlier age. He possessed great dexterity in logically arranging the most difficult themes under discussion and in enforcing his views, even if they were by no means always the most correct." But throughout his life he remained convinced that his opinions always *were* "the most correct". How though, was it possible for him to escape priggishness, brought up as he was in that dull petty Court with its ridiculous etiquette and "minute twaddle", as Leopold called it? And so life went on pleasantly enough until Albert was seventeen, when Fate—in the person of Uncle Leopold—began to take a hand in his affairs.

The luck of Leopold in the marriage market, followed by that of Prince Ferdinand, convinced the Coburg family that, small beer as they were in the comity of nations (not that they would have acknowledged it!) they had a decidedly marketable product in their youthful princelings. Despite their poverty, they did not believe in birth restriction, and their wives were encouraged to be "as the fruitful vine". Their chief ambition was now to marry Albert to his cousin Victoria. Belgium was all very well; so, too, was Portugal; but the Throne of England—ah, that was quite another kettle of fish! England, too, was a Protestant country, which, though of no great consequence, simplified matters. They were ready to adopt any country, any language, any creed, provided it advanced their interests. But they had to move warily in the matter during the lifetime of the old King, who had no use for them and lost no opportunity of letting them know it. Leopold, aided by the indispensable Stockmar, made the first move in the game. He arranged for Albert and his brother to pay a private visit to their Aunt Kent at Kensington Palace. King

William, though he was convinced that those pushing Coburgs were up to something, felt obliged to invite them to spend a day at Windsor Castle. He treated them very casually, falling asleep in the middle of dinner.

Victoria liked them; especially Albert. She admired his "large blue eyes, his beautiful nose, and his white teeth". But, after all, he was only a boy of not quite seventeen— three months younger than she was—and the idea of marriage had not yet seriously entered her head. The young Princes remained in England a month, and Albert hated it. He found English Society—which considered the Coburgs far too unimportant to fuss over—cold and oppressive. The motto "early to bed" had been strictly enforced at Coburg, and he could not keep awake after ten o'clock. The elaborate English meals, too, upset his weak stomach. "The climate, the different ways of living, and the late hours do not agree with me," he wrote. "Our dear Aunt is very kind to us, and our cousin also is very amiable." They met the Duke of Wellington, Captain Marryat and Disraeli, whom Albert described as "a vain young Jew with radical opinions". Their visit concluded, they went to Paris, where the easy-going life of Louis Philippe's Court suited them much better than did England.

Leopold was fairly satisfied with the progress made and used all his diplomacy to push the budding romance. Encouraged by him Albert kept up a correspondence with Victoria and from Switzerland sent her some Edelweiss (from the Righi Pass), a scrap of Voltaire's writing and views of Swiss scenery all nicely arranged in a little book.

Victoria came of age on May 24th, 1837, and the happy event was marked by congratulations and presents from the various members of the Coburg family—including Albert. Uncle Leopold's present arrived on May 25th. It was Stockmar! The wily Baron was charged by his master to worm himself into the confidence of the young Princess and, with that subtlety of which he was a past master, to sing the praises of Albert, tell how he was sighing for love of her charms, and keep his image ever before her eyes. Leopold would have preferred to do this in person, had it been possible, but at any rate he could write (and did): and with Stockmar on the spot he felt fairly safe. And so they wove their web, strong in the conviction that they were, as usual, actuated by the highest motives and that the desire of the family to "better itself" had no place in their schemes. How satisfactory to do a good action and, at the same time, increase his influence in England, thought Leopold. Belgium was not all his fancy had painted it. Says Greville a year later: "My brother writes me word from Paris that Leopold is deadly sick of his Belgian Crown, and impatient to abdicate, thinking that it is better to be an English Prince, uncle to the Queen, with £50,000 a year, than to be monarch of a troublesome, vulgar little kingdom which all its neighbours regard with an evil or a covetous eye."

Stockmar did not arrive on the scene any too soon. The old King died within less than a month, and, lo, Victoria was Queen of England. In his letter of congratulation Albert said: "You are now Queen of the mightiest land in

Europe. In your hands lie the happiness of millions. May Heaven assist you and strengthen you with its strength in that high and difficult task. I hope that your reign may be long, happy and glorious, and that your efforts may be rewarded by the thankfulness and love of your subjects."
Not quite eighteen—and at it already!

So well had Stockmar succeeded in ingratiating himself in the Royal favour, that he had been invited to take up his residence in the Palace, and he remained there for fifteen months. He made the fullest use of his opportunities, worming himself into the confidence of everyone of importance (charming even Palmerston) and serving as go-between when the beloved Melbourne could not be by the side of his Royal Mistress. Melbourne considered him "one of the cleverest fellows I have ever met", and Palmerston said he was the one absolutely disinterested man he had ever come across. He was right, and he was wrong. Money, except as a means to an end, played little part in Stockmar's scheme of existence. He was a man with a mission. He dreamed of a united Germany taking a leading place among the nations, and he felt he could best help his ambitions by remaining behind the scenes and pulling strings.

In 1838 things began to move. Victoria, who had by this time become interested in the idea so cleverly and persistently presented to her, suggested that Stockmar should accompany Albert on a tour—in reality a voyage of inspection—and report to her. Stockmar asked nothing better. It would now be strange indeed if his chickens did not come home to roost.

CHAPTER TWO

AND so in 1838 Albert and Stockmar set out for Italy. One learns more about a man by travelling with him for a month or two than by meeting him casually for a year, and this clever schemer of fifty-one soon discovered that his nineteen-year-old pupil would be as wax in his hands. The lad's disposition was thoroughly kind and amiable, and his great desire was to be considered agreeable. Not, however, to women : from his earliest boyhood he had shown a curious dislike to their society and had never had the suspicion of even a boyish attachment to one; much less an affair. His virtue was, indeed, appalling. Not a single vice redeemed it. He was rather delicate; his stomach, especially, was weak, and he was apt to be sick after any unusual excitement—an additional claim to the sympathy of the dyspeptic Baron. He disliked exertion and found it difficult to concentrate his attention on anything for long. This, as Stockmar of course understood, was the result of the deplorable way in which he had been educated. He was mentally tired, though his mind was crammed full of facts which he had a really extraordinary faculty of acquiring and remembering. He would have won endless prizes in those modern newspaper competitions. To be asked for the exact dimensions of St. Peter's, Rome, the drainage system of Jerusalem, or how many people could sleep abreast in the Great Bed of Ware, would have charmed him.

It is curious to note how little this quite intelligent youth got out of his Italian tour. Greville, making it eight years previously, had enjoyed himself immensely. To begin with the latter had what he described as "a childish liking for Catholic pomp". Now, unless you are interested in churches, one of the chief joys of Italy is lost to you. But everything interested Greville; the people themselves, pictures, politics, theatres, scenery, and he has something worth while to say about all of them—always, however, returning to the subject of the Roman Catholic Church, its intense worldliness and its wonderful organization. He found it wholly admirable that in the churches "there is no class distinction", and that they are always open—"not as ours, opened like theatres at stated hours". This last criticism is, of course, no longer valid. He managed to see everything, and travelling was not too easy a hundred years ago. It took him nine hours to ride by coach from London to Dover and four to cross from Dover to Calais. But travel, if more fatiguing, was infinitely more interesting than it is nowadays, for you were indeed in a foreign country once you had crossed a frontier. You can go round the world now and find in every city the same hotel, the same customs and practically the same way of living as in your own country.

Nothing in Italy aroused Albert's enthusiasm. His bigoted Lutheran mind was horrified at the Roman Catholic Church—with its abuses and its gross superstitions; and his youth and his education prevented him from bringing a philosophic mind to bear on the subject. The intense fascination of its long tradition and the beauty of much of its pageantry entirely eluded him. Neither was he touched by the reticent loveliness of the Tuscan landscape nor interested in the ancient customs—then all kept up. He paid the customary visit to the Pope, and they discussed the origin of Greek art. His Holiness considered that it was derived from that of the Etruscans, but Albert put him right, informing him that it had had its inspiration in early Egyptian art. That was, perhaps, the only occasion on which the question has ever been decided! On the whole, Florence, with all its resources, gave him the most satisfaction. The Gallery, he said, "intoxicated him with delight"; he went for long walks in the delightful surrounding country and played on the organ in the "Badia". He was genuinely fond of music and possessed considerable talent for it. The organ was his great love—he said it was a "noble instrument": it brought "all Heaven before his eyes", which was a great consolation to him. He went a good deal into society, and Stockmar was pleased to see this earnest youth forsaking lovely ladies to talk to learned professors. Perhaps the fact that he was rather shy and *gauche* had something to do with it. But he was disappointed in Italy, alike in "climate, scenery, artistic feeling and skill". It was not Coburg.

Perhaps he was depressed by the political conditions prevailing there and by the Italian hatred of Austria, which included everything Teutonic. The tide of Italy's fortunes was then at the lowest ebb it had ever experienced during her long and eventful history. Apart from her imperishable heritage of art, nothing remained to remind her corrupt and apathetic people of the great days of ancient Rome, the might of Venice and the glories of the *Renaissance*. Without power, *prestige* or wealth, she was at the mercy of any of her neighbours strong enough to come and take what they wanted. By the beginning of 1806 Napoleon had conquered all Northern and Southern Italy; in 1808 he formally annexed the Papal States, and the following year the Pope was arrested and kept a prisoner for three years. Napoleon's disasters, however, resulted in the Pope's restoration to power, and he returned to Rome in 1814. Incessant war (and the exactions of the various rulers) had resulted in an appalling state of poverty and misery, and the restored governments, especially Austria, had acted with but little tact and sympathy towards the soldiers and officials of Napoleon's *régime*—pursuing a policy of revenge and oppression instead of conciliation. Perhaps the only exception to this unhappy state of affairs was Tuscany, where the just and lenient rule of the Grand Duke brought happiness and contentment to the people; for, patriotism and political principles notwithstanding, it is a fact that most people live just as contentedly under an alien despotism as under the rule of a fellow countryman, provided that it enables them to live and work in peace and safety.

Albert's disappointment in the Italian tour was not shared by his companion. He was certainly not more—probably less—capable of appreciating the delights Italy offers to the intelligent traveller; but he had gone there to study Albert, not art, and the result of his efforts had been eminently satisfactory. He could hardly have found an instrument more suited to his purpose and to Leopold's—which was to make friends for Germany and advance its interests in every way possible—than this willing receptive youth. Albert's mind was an empty vessel waiting eagerly to be filled from the Well of Knowledge. With infinite tact and patience Stockmar gradually established an ascendancy over him which lasted unbroken to his dying day. The influence of Mephistopheles over Faust; of George Villiers over James I was not more complete.

What was there in this unpolished boorish middle-class doctor of fifty-one that so attracted the nineteen-year-old Albert? It is one of the most puzzling facts in history. The Baron certainly did not use flattery. On the contrary, he never hesitated to find fault with him and criticize him in his heavy sententious German manner, and, far from resenting it, young Telemachus was humbly grateful to his Mentor and invariably promised to be a good boy in future! Stockmar must have possessed to an abnormal extent that strange magnetic power that some people have of attracting others. His personality was undoubtedly a very strong one: Leopold—a far more virile individual than Albert—had yielded to it. The circumstances, too, were favourable: Albert, but for the Baron, was alone in this—to him—unsympathetic land, and Coburg called unto Coburg; but this does not account for the dog-like devotion that Stockmar inspired; it is wholly inexplicable.

Leopold had, before the Italian tour, broached the subject of the marriage to Albert, who, worthy youth that he was, had, as Leopold wrote to Stockmar, "looked at the question from the most elevated and honourable point of view". He had already made the discovery that "troubles must be inseparable from all human positions" and very sensibly thought that, that being the case, he might just as well endure them as Victoria's husband as in some less exalted station in life; only, he said, he did not want to be kept dangling after her for perhaps two or three years and then be told she had changed her mind. There were other fish in the sea, possibly less worthy of the bait, but still worth catching. Needless to say, Stockmar's reports to Leopold were, if not very enthusiastic with regard to Albert's mental powers, quite decided as to his suitability for the post in question. But the difficulty now was Victoria herself. The "blue eyes, the beautiful nose, and the white teeth" had faded from her memory. Why should she marry? She had tasted blood and liked it, and she had no notion of sharing the privileges of her delightful position with anyone else. She was in love with power. "I had a *Great* deal of business to do after dinner," she writes in her diary. "I get so many papers to sign every day, that I always have a *great deal* to do. I *delight* in this work." After the secluded life she had led at Kensington Palace under the thumb of her mother and the prim Lehzen—who so hated Conroy—it was great fun to be Queen; to be surrounded by servile courtiers and safely enfolded in the affectionate homage and solicitude of the fascinating

Melbourne, who was devoted to her. "I never saw her when she was not laughing and moving about," said Harriet Martineau. "At a tragedy and going to dissolve Parliament it was just the same. It was not pleasant to see her, when Macready's *Lear* was fixing all other hearts and eyes, chattering to the Lord Chamberlain and laughing, with her shoulder turned to the stage." She had discussed the subject of Royal marriages with Melbourne in a joking manner. They spoke of Henry VIII and his odd passion for wives, and Victoria pitied "Poor Katharine of Aragon". "How he ill-used her," she said. "He got tired of her," replied Melbourne: "she was a groaning, moaning woman." A husband might easily turn out to be a "groaning, moaning" man; or worse! There is a story of a small boy who ran to his father screaming: "Mummy's fallen into the well; what *shall* we do?" "Leave well alone, my son," said father! That was Victoria's attitude. But it was time she was married. There were not wanting signs of discontentment. After all, it was not for nothing that she was the daughter of the Duchess of Kent; and her father had been notorious for his gallantries. Better a husband than a Conroy. She was not an Elizabeth and might not have carried off virginity with the same *aplomb* as her great predecessor!

Albert was not the only suitor in the field—his most important rival being the Duc de Nemours, son of Louis Philippe. True, he was a Catholic; but that was easily remedied, and an alliance between France and England would have settled many difficulties. Then there were her

31

two English cousins, the sons of the Dukes of Cumberland
and Cambridge, either of whom would have been a far
more acceptable choice in the eyes of her subjects than a
Frenchman or a German. So Leopold felt it was high time
to take the bull by the horns. He dispatched Ernest and
Albert to England with a letter recommending them to
her *bienveillance*. "They are good and honest creatures,
deserving your kindness and *not pedantic*(!) . . . I am
sure that if you have anything to recommend them, they
will learn it from you."

They arrived at Windsor Castle in the evening, and
Victoria received a *coup de foudre*. This time the "blue
eyes, beautiful nose and white teeth" were irresistible. "At
½ past 7 I went to the top of the staircase and received
my 2 dear cousins, Ernest and Albert, whom I found grown
and changed and embellished. It was with some emotion
I beheld Albert who is *beautiful*. . . ."

"I played 2 games at 'tactics' with dear Albert and 2
at 'Fox and Geese'. Stayed up until 20 m. p. 11. A
delightful evening."

"I sat on the sofa with Albert and played at that game
of letters out of which you are to make words and we had
great fun. Albert gave 'pleasure' and when I said to the
people who were puzzling that it was a very common word,
Albert said, 'But not a very common thing,' upon which
Lord M. said, 'Is it truth or honesty?' which made us all
laugh."

The courtship was not a long one. Victoria promptly
proposed to her "dear cousin", and, without even murmur-

ing the customary Victorian phrase, "This is so sudden", he accepted her! "We embraced each other. There was no hesitation on his part. He is perfect in every way," wrote Victoria; and to his eternal credit—for he was never in love with her—she continued to think him "perfect in every way" until the day of his death.

What did Albert think of it all? It is hard to say. There is no doubt that he was dazzled by the possibilities the position opened up for him. Stockmar had done his work well; he had aroused his ambition, made the dry bones live, given him ideas, and all so cleverly that Albert was convinced that the ideas were his own. He had theories on government, education, art, religion, drainage—everything; and what a chance to put them into practice! He was full of good intentions and hastened to tell Stockmar all about it. "A personality which shall win the respect, the love and the confidence of the Queen and the nation must be the groundwork of my position. This personal character gives security for the motives of our actions, so that if errors occur, they will be more easily pardoned on this account, for even the noblest and fairest undertakings fail in securing support to a man who is not capable of inspiring this confidence." Alas! he was soon to learn that he was not the man to inspire it. He already had his doubts. He was quite sure he did not like England, and he shrewdly suspected that England might not like him. Meanwhile, he returned to Coburg, sending Stockmar to London to look after his interests.

Difficulties began at once. The news of the engagement was received with the utmost coldness. Everyone was agreed as to the desirability of the Queen taking a husband, but no one wanted another German at Court; still less a Coburg. If Victoria did not wish to marry the French Prince or one of her English cousins, what was there to prevent her marrying a member of one of the great families? There was no proviso in the Constitution to prevent her doing so; precedents were not wanting, and there is no doubt that had she done so it would have been infinitely better in every way for the country. If she did not get on with Albert, it would lead to foreign complications; and if she did—a far more dangerous contingency—the Germanizing of the Court would inevitably follow. The first unpleasantness arose over Albert's settlement. Victoria's suggestion of £50,000 a year was vigorously opposed by the Tories, who got it reduced to £30,000—to her great annoyance. Even that, most people considered, was £10,000 too much. They quarrelled over his precedence, refusing to define it by statute, and Victoria finally decided the question herself by an exertion of the Royal prerogative. Then Lord Melbourne appointed one of his own staff, George Anson, a man who was prejudiced against the Germans, to be Albert's private secretary. When he heard of the appointment he wrote to Victoria, protesting; "I am leaving my home with all its old associations, all my bosom friends, and going to a country in which everything is new and strange to me—men, language, customs, modes of life, position." No wonder he clung to Stockmar, who, apart from the fascination he exercised over him, had lived in England, and who, he thought, understood the English. The sycophantic Sir Theodore Martin wrote that Stockmar's being a foreigner was a positive advantage: that being so he could better understand England and advise this German Prince "how to become an English Gentleman"! As a matter of fact, neither Albert nor Stockmar ever succeeded in understanding—or sympathizing with—the English. It was a fatal error to allow this German, whose sole interest was to foster every German instinct in his pupil, to dig himself in at the Court. What was needed was an Englishman of sympathetic disposition and high rank to be with him constantly and teach him to forget Coburg.

All these questions being settled *tant mal que bien*, Lord Torrington and Colonel Grey went to Coburg to fetch the bridegroom-elect and take him the Order of the Garter. Perthès, in recording the event, says: "Queen Victoria will find him the right sort of man, and, unless some unlucky fatality interpose, he is sure to become the idol of the English nation—silently to influence the English aristocracy and affect the destinies of Europe." The latter prediction was unfortunately fulfilled, but he never had the faintest influence on the English aristocracy, nor did the nation idolize him; very far from it.

The party had an enthusiastic send-off. The Coburgers were drunk with pride at the honour paid to their little State: hymns were sung, triumphal arches erected, and white-robed maidens defying the January rigours scattered flowers before the young prince. But "be thou chaste as ice, as pure as snow, thou shalt not escape calumny". John Bull's contempt of petty German Courts was to find expression in spreading the kindly report that Albert's luggage consisted chiefly of a collection of empty trunks as he had nothing with which to fill them! They had an extremely rough crossing. Poor Albert was desperately sick; so were his father and brother Ernest.[1] He managed to struggle up to receive the port authorities at Dover and acknowledge the polite greetings of the inhabitants, though in a condition near to collapse. The party reached London on February 8th, and the wedding took place at the Chapel Royal, St. James's, on February 10th, 1840. Leopold's and Stockmar's chickens had justified the hopes built upon them.

From the first Albert was unhappy. He had nothing in common with England and the English, and he was far too intelligent not to realize that he was not welcome. There is nothing more galling than courteously veiled hostility. He was competent and orderly, and he had come to the land of compromise and brilliant makeshifts. Exact and punctilious, he found himself among the most easy-going and casual people in Europe. Caring little for sport, he was expected to take a leading position in a Society that lived for it. Above all, he was utterly destitute of a sense of humour—that blessed gift which has always been the saving grace of the English nation. He had all the qualities of a good conscientious managing clerk, and he was to be

_____
[1] *Et sic omnia!*

the Consort of the Queen. He was, too, a moral prig of the first order, and the drinking habits and somewhat loose lives of the aristocracy horrified him. There must be none of that sort of thing in *his* household! He demanded such moral qualities in his equerries that one gentleman approached "thanked Heaven that his character was much too bad for the job"! "This damned morality will ruin everything," said Melbourne. Victoria was at first inclined to be tolerant and kindly; but not so Albert. *"Nous allons changer tout çela,"* he decided.

Had he been able to laugh at himself things would have been easier for him, but the idea that a Coburg could under any circumstances be a subject for mirth never occurred to him. His appearance was against him. He looked intensely German and spoke English badly, and his expressionless "barber's block" type of beauty was not to the English taste. The "blue eyes, beautiful nose and white teeth" so admired by Victoria were combined with a somewhat slouching carriage; his manners were self-conscious, cold and stiff; he spoke to members of the Household with the air of a schoolmaster dealing with rather stupid boys, and he had that passion for etiquette which was then common to all the members of those petty little German Courts whose whole stock-in-trade was their rank. In all his life no one—outside his own family— had ever told him exactly what they thought of him. "Neither man nor woman can be worth anything," said Melbourne, "until they have discovered that they are fools. This is the first step towards becoming either estimable or agreeable, and until it be taken there is no hope." This discovery Albert never made; and he was, too, very far from realizing that by the English aristocracy a German Prince was considered as of little more importance than an English knight. The great families in those days kept up tremendous state and were superbly arrogant. When in mid-nineteenth century Lord Ashburnham was dying, he sent for the village clergyman to speed him on his journey and was furious that the poor man had dared to come to the front entrance!

This was all very trying to a young man who was convinced that his mission in life was to impress and improve everyone with whom he came in contact.

His brother Ernest, who remained in England for three months—a more worldly-wise though less admirable person than Albert—very soon saw how little he was fitted for English life. He wrote after Albert's death: "For my own part, my stay at the English Court afforded me many experiences, so that I was able much better to understand English life and character. Indeed, the peculiarities of English society found from the first more sympathy in me than in my brother. The passion of the high nobility for every kind of sport found more echo and comprehension in me than in him, and thus I gained fuller access to the Englishman's reserved heart. I will not decide if Prince Albert ever was able to strike the true chord in his dealings with the nation. I had many an argument with him on the subject and always felt that his was a hard lot in having to live in harmonious intelligence with that great Island race." He goes on to say that on one occasion, when they were riding together and Albert had been criticizing English life and customs pretty freely, he turned to him, saying: "When you are gone I shall have no one to exchange an unrestrained word with about these things. An Englishman does not understand or enter into these matters and would only see the foreigner's love of fault-finding." He never lost this flattering opinion of us. But happily he had Stockmar—now settled comfortably in the Palace—to teach him "how to be an English Gentleman" and also an extra secretary, a German, who had been secretary to the Duchess of Kent, and whom the outspoken Ernest describes as "a worthy man, but with all the failings of a German Philistine". And he had Victoria, who became every day more infatuated with him. He was already "My dearest Angel".

CHAPTER THREE

BUT, in spite of Victoria and Stockmar, Albert found life very difficult at first. Much as she adored her "dearest Angel", she was not yet inclined to share anything with him except the Royal Bed. Perhaps, indeed, her resentment at the reduction of the proposed settlement was due rather to the fact that it was a slight to her personally than to any concern on Albert's account. She wanted a loving husband, but he must remember that his wife was Queen of England and that £30,000 a year, although less than she had asked for him, was still equal to the total revenue of Coburg. He was Lord of her heart—but of nothing else. This was the more trying, as constant association with Stockmar was changing the somewhat purposeless youth into a portentously serious young man anxious to make his presence felt in the country of his adoption. His prudent German soul was shocked at the waste and extravagance he saw around him. The running of the Royal Household was divided among the officers of State and was regulated on almost medieval lines. The maidservants were under the Chamberlain, the footmen under the Master of the Horse, and the cooks under the Lord Steward, who was also responsible for providing fuel and laying the fires, which, however, he must not light, as that duty was fulfilled by the Lord Chamberlain. It was, perhaps, the most uncomfortable

BARON FREDERICK STOCKMAR

house in England. Albert remonstrated and was politely ignored. He was only a meddlesome foreigner. Stockmar drew up an elaborate memorandum on the subject written with such heavy gravity that it was almost humorous, but it was not until two years later, when Albert had come into his own, that his recommendations were adopted and the whole domestic arrangements placed in the hands of one official—responsible only to Albert. The saving effected was enormous.

English life did not grow on him. He disliked the people, saying that they were cold and reserved. How different it all was from Coburg, where he knew everyone and was met everywhere with friendly guttural greetings. The English Sunday, too, bored him to death. He must take England in hand and try to improve these savage Islanders!

Things would have been pleasanter for him had he been a little more tactful. Soon after his marriage, he was invited to dine with the Lord Mayor and Corporation on receiving the freedom of the City. He declined at first, but afterwards agreed to be present. The Duke of Cambridge wrote to him saying that as he (Albert) was not used to those ceremonies he might perhaps be of service to him. Albert did not reply and, when they met at the Mansion House, begged the Duke as a favour not to stay to dinner as he himself had changed his mind and decided not to do so. The Duke told him he could do as he liked, but that he (the Duke) should certainly stay. After Albert's departure the Lord Mayor told the Duke that everyone was so indignant at his rudeness that he was afraid they would all turn down their glasses when his health was proposed. The Duke very good-naturedly tried to smooth things over and made a speech in which he said that they must excuse Albert, as he had "just married a fine young girl, and that they were fond of each other's company". Far from being grateful, both Albert and the "fine young girl" were furious that the Duke had dared to stay to dinner after Albert had requested him not to do so.

Stockmar took full advantage of Albert's rather lonely and isolated position to strengthen his already almost complete ascendancy over him. He urged patience, suggested endless ways in which he might gradually make his influence felt, instructed him in statecraft and, above all, discussed the unhappy condition of the Fatherland under its innumerable petty rulers hating each other and torn by dissensions. What could a united Germany under the rule of Prussia, its most efficient and strongest State, not accomplish in civilizing and educating benighted Europe? As the Baron, speaking in the dear German tongue, pictured his Utopia, Albert saw visions of a new Holy Land illuminating the dark places of the earth with the brightness of its arising, while Righteousness and Peace—and *Kultur*—kissed each other. And *he* would have helped to call it into being. Ah—that would, indeed, be something worth working for ! He was only twenty-one, and it was a romantic age.

They were both of them perfectly sincere and convinced of the utter superiority of the German race over all others. And, that being the case, a close collaboration between

England and Germany could not fail to benefit both countries. Then, too, it would be the means of keeping those odious French in their place. Certainly Napoleon had not succeeded in making his country loved.

Alas! dreams die at the opening day, and in the meanwhile Albert was very uncomfortable. He hated late hours more than ever, and London did not agree with him. He was happy only when he could escape to Windsor and wander in the Forest. Victoria, on the other hand, liked all the gaiety and glitter of Court life. She loved dancing and had no interest in any kind of intellectual or artistic pursuit. Artists and musicians were all very well in their way; it was part of her duty—and pleasure—to encourage the arts, but she saw no reason why "people of that sort" should be unduly fussed over. She would have highly disapproved of the Society that Lorenzo de'Medici delighted in gathering round him; indeed, she would soon have nipped the Renaissance in the bud! So Albert had to give up his idea of forming a Royal Salon where famous and deferential musicians, painters, literary men and scientists should meet and learn his ideas on their respective *métiers*. All his life he consoled himself, when worried, with his beloved organ. Lady Lyttelton writes in 1850: "From an open window below this floor began suddenly to sound the Prince's organ,[1] expressively played by his masterly hand. Such a modulation! minor and solemn, and ever-changing

---

[1] The fine instrument which Albert had caused to be removed from the Pavilion at Brighton and set up in the ballroom at Buckingham Palace.

and never ceasing. From a *piano* like Fanny Lind's swelling note up to the fullest swell, and still the same fine vein of melancholy! And it came on so exactly as an accompaniment to the sunset. How strange he is! He must have been playing while the Queen was finishing her toilet. And then he went to cut jokes and eat dinner and no one but the organ knows what is in him!" Lady Lyttelton's musical metaphors are rather mixed, but she evidently sensed poor Albert's unhappiness.

It is, perhaps, not surprising that Albert did not like England. True, he had Stockmar and the adoring Victoria, but there was nothing in the life of the Court either to interest or amuse him. Victoria's idea of spending a happy evening was either to dance or to play round games with the guests and the Ladies and Gentlemen in Waiting, and he could not but be aware that the high officials of the Household and the aristocracy were, though civil enough, keeping him at arm's length. England, even under the best conditions, has never been a particularly agreeable country for a foreigner. A hundred years ago it was unbelievably insular, and, to a cultured stranger, perhaps a little uncivilized. The upper classes were a curious mixture of coarseness and refinement. Many of the men were excellent classical scholars—the public schools and Universities saw to that—but their chief amusements were shooting, hunting and gambling, and they were hard drinkers. The poorer classes were poor indeed. Greville writes: "Poverty and vice and misery must always be found in a community like ours, but such frightful contrasts between the excess of luxury and these scenes of starvation and brutality ought not to be possible. I am afraid there is more vice, more misery, more penury in this country than in any other, and, at the same time, greater wealth."

A hundred years ago the English laws were almost as savage as they were in Tudor times; Equity had hardly any meaning, and Justice was very blind. They were the days of the "Bow Street Runners", of poor "Miss Flite" who expected a judgment only on "the Day of Judgment", and of "Jarndyce and Jarndyce". People were imprisoned for debt and kept there until the debt was paid. A man could be hanged for stealing goods of the value of five pounds; but juries were more humane than the law and, whatever the value of the property stolen, generally declared it to be of the value of four pounds nineteen shillings only. Transportation was in full swing: children could be transported for stealing a loaf of bread. There were no fixed working hours. Children of eight worked twelve hours a day in coal-mines, starting work at four in the morning. When Victoria came to the throne sweeps still went their rounds accompanied by their poor little climbing boys, but this ghastly abuse was abolished in 1841. The drinking was appalling. Beer was the chief beverage; even in the late 'fifties many university undergraduates still drank it at breakfast, and at breakfast-parties the tankard was passed round as a finish to the feast. Gin, too, was highly popular. In London the big gin-shops were each visited by about three thousand customers a day, and in Edinburgh there was one for every fourteen families. Many of these drinking-shops had placards in their windows announcing that you could get drunk for a penny and blind drunk for twopence. The streets were full of drunken men and women and prostitutes. The amusements of the people had changed little since the days of Charles II. Bull and bear-baiting still went on, and there were cock-fights, dog-fights and badger drawings. Boxing was brutal, and victories were frequently arranged in advance. There was very little education for the working-class—apart from the Church Schools—and the children of the very poor were not educated at all. People still travelled by coach—railways were in their infancy—and in London you drove in hackney-cabs and cabriolets. The Government was entirely in the hands of the upper classes. The large middle class, which was only just coming into being, included bankers, lawyers and doctors. Even the richest merchants and manufacturers were considered to rank merely as superior tradespeople—though, of course, there were always exceptions to the general rule. London was then a very small city compared with the huge unwieldy London of to-day. Kensington Palace as Victoria knew it was the great house of a country village, and Hampstead and the southern suburbs were quite rural.

The Prince of Wales was born on November 9th, 1841, and by this time Albert's position was very different from what it had been eighteen months previously. Victoria had discovered where true joys were to be found and lived only for her "dearest Albert". He had begun to infect her with his own dislike of late hours and town life, and it was now her greatest joy to get up early and walk in Windsor Forest with him before breakfast. During her confinement she ordered the dispatch-boxes from the Foreign Office to be sent to him, and from that period he began to write those interminable memoranda on every conceivable subject, the composing of which became a veritable passion with him. Under Stockmar he was making great progress and beginning to gain a real grasp of political questions. If, after learning his views, Her Majesty's Ministers acted on their own—well—that was another matter. Sir Theodore Martin, however, tells us that Melbourne, Peel and Lord Aberdeen hung on his words—"they all felt that they were in safe hands: that he would never betray them, show up their foibles, their errors, their faults, or play off one political man against another", which was, of course, very nice for Her Majesty's Ministers. But, whether they liked it or not, they were obliged to take the memoranda seriously, for the views set forth therein were often extremely sound. The hand was indeed the hand of Albert, but the voice was the voice of Stockmar. And the little sallow dyspeptic Baron was an extraordinarily able man, whose views on almost any subject were worth hearing, and whose knowledge of statesmanship was probably unique in Europe. He was now more firmly entrenched than ever; rooms were reserved for him both at Buckingham Palace and Windsor; he came and went as he chose, and Court etiquette did not exist for him. He refused to wear Court dress, on the grounds that silk stockings and knee-breeches would not sufficiently protect his legs and he might catch cold. One wonders what Victoria would have said had Peel—or even the beloved Melbourne—ventured to make the same excuse. Albert hung on his lightest word or gesture, and he was the virtual ruler of the Household. He was consulted on every detail in connection with it: medicine, charities, servants, governesses, place-seekers, education; nothing came amiss to him. "The nursery gives me more trouble than the Government of a Kingdom," he wrote *à propos* of the birth of Princess Victoria. "Inquire within upon Everything" might have been written on the door of his suite.

It is curious that Victorian Ministers should not have realized how unwise it was to allow this middle-class German to pull so many strings, but one must remember that at this period Germany was very "small beer" among the nations. One German more or less—what did it matter? It was not so with the people, who were very suspicious with regard to his activities. The Press, too, insulted him, calling him "the intriguing Stockmar, the agent of the Jesuit Leopold", and so on. These rumours were so widespread that the Speaker of the House of Commons, Mr. Abercromby, told the Prime Minister that he felt it was his duty to call attention in Parliament to the unconstitutional position of the foreigner, Stockmar. The easy-going Melbourne pointed out that he was useful in filling a gap caused by certain circumstances. He told Stockmar what was being said, who answered, "Tell Abercromby to bring forward the motion against me in Parliament. I shall know how to defend myself."

Melbourne tactfully contrived to have the question dropped. He did not, of course, wish to have the matter discussed publicly, and it was naturally the last thing in the world that Stockmar desired. Melbourne knew very well with whom he had to deal and said afterwards: "King Leopold and Stockmar are very good intelligent people, but I dislike very much to hear it said by my friends that I am influenced by them." The knowledge that—except by Albert and, therefore, by Victoria—he was not loved in no wise troubled him. He went hardly at all into general society, and he had—that supreme necessity of the political schemer—the hide of a rhinoceros. His health, however, was wretched; he suffered agonies from heartburn, which made meals a misery to him. And poor Albert's "Little Mary" grew weaker and weaker. Two stomachs that ached as one!

But, whatever the state of his digestion, Stockmar "never relaxed"—to use his favourite motto: nor did he allow his pupil to do so. It would have been better had they taken a holiday during the exciting days when the little Prince was born, leaving the arrangements for the christening in other hands. Albert muddled them badly, Greville tells us. When the birth was expected hourly, he put off sending word to the dignitaries whose duty it was to be present until so late that several of them, including the Archbishop of Canterbury, arrived after the event. Then, too, they showed their German proclivities a little too plainly. The child was not allowed a single English godparent. The choice of the King of Prussia, who came to England for the occasion, was naturally extremely unpopular. "The King," we are told, "formed a strong friendship with both the Queen and her husband." It was another step in the forward march of the Fatherland. Again, when the question of the Prince of Wales's armorial bearings was discussed, Albert and Victoria wanted to quarter the arms of Saxony with the Royal arms, and they gazetted the little boy "Duke of Saxony". This passion for everything German caused intense irritation in the country. Had they taken responsible English advice, instead of leaning entirely on the arch-German Stockmar, such mistakes could not have been made. Greville is very frank on the subject, and no one was in a better position to know all that was going on than he was. Lord Malmesbury, too, said, "Even the closest friends of the Court never overlooked his (Albert's) German proclivities and temperament."

Stockmar's chief friend in the Royal Household was Albert's German secretary, Dr. Prätorius, and, afterwards, his successor, Carl Meyer—a Jew—both of whom the Baron influenced and protected, seeing to it that they were careful to foster the Prince's German sympathies. Prätorius was an extraordinarily ugly man; and when, as Victoria was one day reading the Bible to the little Princess Royal, they came to the passage: "And God created man in His own image" —"But surely not Dr. Prätorius, dear Mamma," said the child.

Albert, perhaps because of the depression caused by his poor digestive powers, luxuriated in woe. He was largely responsible for the *culte* of deep mourning in Victorian days. And he taught Victoria to mourn, too! So well, that for years after his death she signed herself, in writing to her children, "Your unhappy Mamma" and kept his rooms exactly as he had left them, giving orders that his clothes were to be laid out every evening and hot water taken to his dressing-room. When his father died in 1844, he was quite annoyed that the English public did not share in his grief for this—to them—almost unknown Coburg Duke. He writes: "Here we sit together, 'poor Mamma, Victoria, and myself', and weep, with a great cold public around us, insensible as a stone. With him it is well. I share your belief that his would have been a dreary old age, and even were not my faith strong in the Providence which shapes all things for our good, I should find consolation in this. Still, for us the loss is terrible." Why so terrible for Victoria? She had not seen very much of him, and the relations between Albert and his father had not been too agreeable. The Duke had felt, with regard to his son's lucky marriage, "It is a gift by whatsoever thou mightest be profited to me," and Albert, who was of a frugal mind, was not anxious to shower largess on his family. In his letter of condolence to his brother Ernest, after telling him that "Victoria weeps with me, and our poor little ones ask us why we are in black", he promises "always to be ready with *advice*"! Poor Anson, who had neither liked nor approved of the Duke of Coburg, was so upset by Albert's floods of tears that he retired to bed with a nervous headache. (How often, by the way, we read in Victorian literature of these devastating nervous headaches! They were probably due to the heavy food and wines, stuffy rooms and dislike of fresh air.) It was the same thing when his valet "Kart" died. "I burst into tears," says Albert, and "tears rushed to Victoria's eyes all day". He was capable of weeping over the death of a rich aunt!

His brother Ernest criticized him frankly but, on the whole, kindly. He seemed to have considered him a man of contradictions—aren't we all?—but few, perhaps, to the same extent. "His gentle amiability," he says, "was really coupled with such a critical sternness as to be almost a psychological riddle. The great self-sacrificing affection sometimes was changed into painful coldness, and he was often on the borders of that dangerous temptation (to those in powerful and exalted positions) of imparting views and motives suggested by contempt of mankind. Yet never in my life have I met with anyone who had so pure a sympathy for humanity in the abstract." *"In the abstract."* Ah, there's the rub! We have all met those lofty-minded persons who can sympathize deeply with their fellow-men *en masse*. An earthquake in Japan will rouse all their best instincts, and yet they can be strangely cold and untouched by the troubles of those who immediately surround them. Ernest goes on to say that it was his brother's perpetual thought how to make men happy, "and yet he could be very hard on an individual man"—he didn't like lending Ernest money!—"His keen logical understanding came into full play, and with unmerciful argument he pulled to pieces other people's opinions and actions. . . ." The weakness of men and their doings came more sharply and strongly before his judgment than it did to others; the battle of life rendered him more severe and opinionated in his conclusions. As he became more wrapped up in his own doctrines, he lost much of his natural cheerfulness and pleasure in his own vocations. "I am far from maintaining," he says, "that it was by English life and manners that my brother's nature became morbid with 'the pale cast of thought', but a passage in a letter to King Leopold in connection with a different subject illustrates what I mean. 'An Englishman does not know what to be *froh* means. When they laugh, it is to see a fellow-citizen torn to pieces.'" A more gotesquely false and unfair judgment of the English could hardly have been formed, but it was typical of the man. There was undoubtedly a certain subtle antagonism between Albert and the English, which completely froze up all friendliness and geniality in their relations and effectually prevented any possibility of their understanding one another. Ernest considers that Stockmar was partly responsible for Albert's depression and says that "with much loftiness of thought in Stockmar's circle, there was also engendered a narrowness of spirit almost leading to claims of infallibility". Well . . . plain living and high thinking can be very trying!

CHAPTER FOUR

IF Albert's popularity with Her Majesty's subjects was not
increasing, he reigned supreme in the heart of Victoria
herself. He was now, too, not only her "dearest Angel";
he was also her "dearest Master"—a new and significant
development, this. She had already reached the happy state
of mind of which she wrote in 1852, "Albert grows fonder
and fonder of politics and business, and is so wonderfully
fit for both—such perspicacity and such *Courage*!—and I
grow daily to dislike both more and more. We women
are not *made* for governing—and if we are *Good* women,
must dislike these masculine occupations, but there are times
which force one to take *interest* in them, *malgré, bon gré,*
and I do, of course, intensely." Albert, on his part, described
himself playfully as "the husband of the Queen, the tutor
of the Royal children, the private secretary of the sovereign
and her permanent minister". He was all that, and he
might well have added, *and King of her Realms*, for such
he was to all intents and purposes. Every State document
was submitted to him, and no question which came within
the provenance of the Queen was decided without him.
Her Majesty's Ministers accepted this state of affairs with
as good a grace as they might—they could not very well
do otherwise—and waded through the enormously long
memoranda on every conceivable subject which Albert so
delighted in writing. Lytton Strachey gives us an interest-

ing picture of his indefatigable industry and shows him at early dawn sitting at his desk with the green-shaded lamp, writing, writing, writing, while Victoria—who, poor thing, no longer chased the glowing hours with flying feet—sat beside him deciding affairs of State or, rather, listening to *his* decisions and drinking in the words of wisdom that fell from his lips.

The situation was not without its pathos. This young man had not yet reached the age of thirty, but he had long since lost all wish to enjoy himself, and alas! his depression —which now amounted almost to a disease—had infected Victoria also and, like a deadly miasma, was spreading over the whole Court circle and thence over the country at large. Life is short, say the young, and "Youth's a stuff will not endure". "It is good and comely for one to eat and to drink, and to enjoy the good of all his labour that he taketh under the sun." Life is short, said Albert, and you cannot eat and drink with any satisfaction, if good cheer makes you sick. "Work while it is day, for the night cometh when no man can work." So he immolated himself on the altar of duty, forgetting—to quote again the words of the Preacher—that "there is no remembrance of the wise more than of the fool for ever; seeing that which now is, in the days to come, shall all be forgotten". There was so much to do; and those arrogant easy-going English were so slack and casual. The times were out of joint; but, far from feeling that any cursed spite had caused him to be born to set them right, he congratulated Providence on its far-seeing wisdom.

The great thorn in the flesh of both Victoria and Albert was Lord Palmerston. With most of the Ministers Albert's relations, if not cordial, were correct, but what could you do with a man like that, who decided weighty affairs in the light of his immediate inspiration, writing but little and—Albert shrewdly suspected—leaving his (Albert's) memoranda unread! He (the egregious Palmerston) even made light of Stockmar, treating this formidable Royal favourite much as he might have treated an honest *employé*. How they hated him! After his death Albert described him as "the man who has embittered our whole lives". A remarkable man and one whom you could not ignore. He was as popular with the nation as Albert was unpopular. There is an excellent portrait of him in "Random Recollections of the Lords and Commons, 1838". The writer does not like him apparently, saying: "His talents are by no means of a high order. He is very irregular in his attendance on his Parliamentary duties, and, when in the House, is by no means active in defence either of his principles or his friends. Scarcely anything calls him up except a regular attack on himself, or on the way in which the department of the public service with which he is entrusted is administered. In person Lord Palmerston is tall and handsome. His face is round and of a darkish hue. His hair is black, and always exhibits proofs of the skill and attention of the *perruquier*. His clothes are in the extreme of fashion. He is very vain of his personal appearance, and is generally supposed to devote more of his time in sacrificing to the Graces than is consistent with the duties of a person who has so much to do with the destinies of Europe. Hence it is that *The Times* newspaper has fastened on him the *soubriquet* of 'Cupid'."

The rise of Albert had meant also that of Stockmar: indeed, had it not been for the wily Baron, it is doubtful if Albert would ever have been anything more than the husband of the Queen. *His* were the opinions embodied in the Memoranda; from *him* originated the dreary moral priggishness that infected the Court, and *his* was the still small voice bidding Albert to "never relax". He came and went as he chose, coming, unfortunately, more than he went, and such was his insolent certainty of the power he wielded that he did not even trouble to inform his hosts of his departures or pay them the common courtesy of taking leave. And, far from resenting this impertinence, Victoria, with all her overweening sense of her own importance, and Albert, that walking book of Etiquette, bombarded him with letters imploring him not to leave them comfortless and desolate! "Alas!" writes Victoria; "the inestimable, good, dear Stockmar, gone without a word! My poor Albert!" Yet she would crush with devastating coldness the least slight to her Royal dignity on the part of one of the Court circle. Albert writes, after one of the Baron's rude flittings, "Come, as you love me, as you love Victoria, as you love *Uncle Leopold*, as you love your *German Father-land*!" And on another occasion: "I will send after you only one word of the dismay occasioned by your sudden disappearance. There was an outcry throughout the house from great and small, young and old! 'The Baron is gone.'

Then, however, came variations upon it. 'I wanted to say this and this to him'—'He promised he would stay longer'—'I went to his room and found it empty'—'I would have travelled with him'—'He promised to carry a letter to my father'—*'J'ai encore commencé un travail qu'il demandait'*.

"You can divine who were the persons by what they exclaimed, without my naming them; but not the feelings of regret which overwhelmed all at having lost you from among us."

Perhaps, after all, Royalties like being treated like this: it is such a novelty for them. They are hardly ever contradicted. How good, by the way, would the give and take of the brilliant conversation at Holland House have been for Albert! He needed contradiction. The incidence of birth and the exigencies and etiquette of Court life combine to render Royal personages less intelligent than they might be, and the more intellectual among them must be conscious of this. The deference they demand causes men who are leaders in their own sphere of knowledge to defer to men like Albert, who have, as schoolboys say, swotted up the subject in order to be able to converse upon it, and —such is human vanity and weakness—the experts are often flattered at being noticed! In the great days of the Renaissance it was not so. The aristocracy of genius—the only genuine aristocracy—was valued at its true worth. Queen Victoria was in no way intellectual. Her knowledge of literature was slight, her taste in art deplorable. She had no conversation, no wit and but little sense of humour, and yet in her youth we find the brilliant Melbourne her slave and, in later years, the equally brilliant Beaconsfield at her feet. Quite clever women, too, Lady Lyttelton and Lady Bloomfield among them, record her most banal remarks as if they were sallies of a Congreve or a Wilde.

When the Baron *did* happen to be paying one of his rare visits to his disconsolate family—who seem to have supported his continual absence with much greater equanimity than did Albert—they corresponded. How they corresponded! Interminable memoranda full of copy-book maxims and the moral platitudes—not only of Victorian days—but of *all* time arrived at the Palace every day. Albert existed for them and wrote even longer replies, enclosing for his tutor's inspection the memoranda he proposed inflicting on Her Majesty's Ministers and the still more dreary speeches he had prepared for delivery at the various functions at which he had been asked to speak.

As was only natural, the education of the young Prince of Wales passionately interested both Albert and the Baron. At first "Bertie" was allowed to live the normal life of the children of the great, under the kindly care of Lady Lyttelton; but this could not go on. Bertie must be *Educated*. Our Albert could think of nothing better than the same system of which he himself was so admirable a product. And the relentless Baron agreed, only insisting that it must be still more severe—seeing the exalted position the boy was one day to occupy. Neither of them, unfortunately, had the faintest understanding of the child mind. The child has nowadays come fully into his own

—and a little of his elder's, too!—but at that period the phrase "You're only a child" was heard every moment and was intended to make children realize the utter insignificance of their lowly state and lead them to a proper appreciation of the wisdom, power and goodness of the adult! Only a child! That shy wild sensitive loving little being—compact with vivid imagination and practical common sense: If only Albert and Stockmar had selected at random three or four boys from any preparatory school and taken them out to tea once a week or so, yielding themselves up to the delightful companionships of their little guests, it might have helped to humanize them—that is, if they *could* have relaxed. As we have seen, however, the word "relax" had no place in the Baron's vocabulary.

There was some talk of asking Wilberforce to undertake "Princey's" education, and Lady Lyttelton prayed that it might come about. The experiment could not have lasted long, as the kindly child-loving Archdeacon would have rebelled at inflicting "the system" on his poor little charge, while, being a courtier born, he would have been equally anxious to comply with the Royal wishes. Wilberforce certainly did not meet with the approval of Stockmar, who worked tooth and nail to get his own way. Memoranda of portentous gravity and length were drawn up on the subject, and Stockmar wrote: "I have for months pursued my plan with unflagging obstinacy. I could not do this without rendering myself odious, but the difficulties in the way could not stop me. The result is that there is now every prospect that nine-tenths of my proposals will be adopted." The Royal couple were humbly grateful to him, Victoria feeling that the system that had produced Albert must indeed be a perfect one. Had the "system" justified the hopes and expectations built upon it, "Bertie" would have grown up an engaging combination of King Arthur, Woodrow Wilson and Martin Tupper!

"Education," said Melbourne, "does not do so much as is expected from it; it may mould and direct the character, but it rarely alters it." It had little chance either way with "Bertie", for alas! "Bertie" refused to be educated! The more he was led to the Fountain of Knowledge the more he disliked its waters. "Stay me with flagons, comfort me with apples, for I am sick of . . . education!" said "Bertie"; so, on the whole, the "system" did less harm than might have been expected. Lady Lyttelton, warm-hearted and sensible, thoroughly disliked severity and repression towards children. Speaking of the advice Victorian parents were so fond of giving their children at meal-times to "always leave off eating while you are still hungry", she writes that "you might as well say, 'When you are washing, always leave off dirty' "!

The Royal couple allowed themselves very few relaxations. One of their greatest pleasures was to escape to Osborne, the estate which they had bought out of the savings effected through the reform of the Household. There they would walk in the woods and pretend they were peasants —à la Marie Antoinette and her ladies, who, at Versailles, played at being milkmaids. They had each a Japan box, one marked V.R. and the other A. These they would fill with small pieces of wood and twigs to burn in their apartments. Music, which had once occupied much of their time, was rather neglected. In the early days of their marriage Victoria had been very fond of singing. She had even honoured the Court by taking part in a State concert and singing five numbers, including a duet with Albert and a trio with Rubini and Lablache. They still played duets together. At one of those musical evenings in which they so delighted they played Beethoven's Septet, arranged for two pianos and four performers, and Victoria said, when they reached the last bar, "What a relief to find we have all finished together!"

Albert was genuinely musical. Music was, perhaps, the subject he best understood and for which he was the most fitted, and, had he not been cursed with Stockmar, he might have done much for it in England. His taste was excellent. He knew and loved the best works of Bach and Beethoven long before they were generally known and appreciated in England, and—which is even more remarkable—he was a lover of that greatest of polyphonic composers, Palestrina. Of Gluck he wrote: "We have seen the 'Orpheus' (Gluck's) twice, and I admire it extremely. It is a real refreshment after our modern sound and fury and the works of the Italian school, which depend entirely on *morceaux* and have no regard whatever to the poetry of the drama." I wonder how many musicians in England at that period have ever heard Gluck's "Orfeo" or were aware that his was not the only setting of the lovely old legend. Victoria had a touching admiration for everything Albert did: "At dinner," says Lady Lyttelton, "the incomparable band of the 1st Life Guards played, quite to admiration, a piece of solemn choral music, which one saw all round the table people stopping their talk to listen to and feel—so perfectly from the usual style; but it was, indeed, most beautiful, and the Queen called to me in a low voice and with a great blush: "Don't you like that? It is composed by the Prince."

How much happier would Albert have been if, instead of worrying the Cabinet with his incessant memoranda and insisting on pushing his way where he was neither needed nor wanted, he had devoted his attention and his musical intelligence to the service of the art he loved! We might easily have had a first-class endowed Opera in London and permanent orchestras in all the great towns. Victoria would have backed him up in anything he undertook during his lifetime and would have continued her support after his death in his memory. The impetus and influence would have been principally German, but it was that to a great extent already. The musical Germanization of England was begun by Handel, and the process continued through the Court influence and the enormous *culte* of Mendelssohn. Albert, however, was by no means musically bigoted. His taste, on the contrary, was extremely Catholic. He would have delighted in drawing up a scheme for a state opera and would doubtless have taken care that its scope was not too narrow. No country has done more for music than Germany; and no country has done it more harm. It was responsible for the "Four-Square" tunes, which dominated

European music for so many years, and also for the overwhelming influence of Wagner which sterilized so much promising talent. Had it not been for Germany, English music might have continued the tradition of the great Church composers and madrigalists of the Tudor period.

But with Stockmar ever at hand—whether at Buckingham Palace, Windsor or Osborne—whispering his ambitions into the ear of poor Albert, what was there for him to do except to go on working always harder and harder, struggling with the aggravating Palmerston and the exigencies of his rapacious and ambitious family? He was dog tired, and his health was far from satisfactory. Victoria, too, was tired. No wonder, considering the constant succession of babies and the strain of official duties—made harder by Albert's exactions: for, kind and affectionate as he was, he had no more mercy on her than he had on himself. What a wonderful wife she was! Truly regal on public occasions, exacting every iota of the deference she considered her due. Feared by her family—and a formidable nut for her Ministers to crack—with Albert she was as humble and pliable as the little wife of a small city clerk, serving, watching over and loving her man. She set the example of wifely submission to her subjects, and the great middle-class, who saw in this Royal *ménage* a reflection of the lives they themselves led, were quick to follow it. Where are they to be found now, those mid-Victorian wives content to bring up large families and do uncomplainingly the endless work of the mid-nineteenth century household? They made their own bread and preserves, washed their dirty linen at home—in more senses than one—sewed, darned and mended. One best dress sufficed them for a year; and an occasional visit to the theatre, a yearly holiday at the seaside—always at the same place—and such small social amenities as their means allowed them were all they asked of life. Dull perhaps, you will say, in comparison with the relaxations that the Twentieth Century with its picture-houses, bridge, cheap motors, golf and tennis offers to the same class? Possibly; but what you have never had you do not miss, and when pleasures and excitements were rare they were enjoyed in anticipation and in retrospect in a way which would bring a pitying smile to the faces of the nervous restless young people of to-day, to whom an evening at home is the abomination of desolation. Well—*autre temps, autre mœurs*. We are enjoying the fruits of modern progress and, incidentally, paying rather heavily for them.

The marital relations of Victoria and Albert were an excellent example for "Bertie". Perhaps, like the "system", the motto "be good" was too strictly enforced, for rumours credited him with less moral rigidity than that of his father. When married he was always exquisitely courteous to his charming wife—and rather afraid of her. Queen Alexandra considered that time was made for slaves and was notoriously unpunctual. There was an amusing story told in Court circles of an occasion when they had to catch a train and she was taking—as usual—an abnormally long time to dress. Word was sent to her two or three times to no effect.

"We shall miss the train, Sir," said Sidney Greville. King Edward, fuming and fretting, answered: "It's really *intolerable*. I'll go myself and hurry her." As he approached her room, his footsteps grew slower and slower, and when he reached it he paused nervously and, tapping gently, asked in a meek voice: "Aren't you nearly ready, dear? I am afraid we shall miss the train!" She was always at *least* half or three quarters of an hour late for dinner, and His Majesty used to sit on a chair outside her door gently beseeching her to hasten her *toilette*.

Albert's moral priggishness was strikingly shown in the unfortunate Somerset affair in 1843, when the same mistake was made as in the notorious case of Lady Flora Hastings— a mistake that could not have occurred had Albert had any other adviser than Stockmar. Lady Augusta Somerset was credited with having had a love affair with Prince George of Cambridge, and it was even reported that she was *enceinte*. Both the young people indignantly denied the truth of the rumours concerning them, but Victoria and Albert, with real Christian charity, believed the worst. Victoria even discussed the scandal with the Duchess of Gloucester, who insisted on her putting in writing the statements she had made verbally, sending the document to the Duchess of Cambridge. Both the Duke and Duchess took the matter up vigorously, and Victoria and Albert had to climb down, which they did both reluctantly and ungraciously, Albert writing: "that, as Prince George had given his word of honour that the story was not true, he *supposed* they must believe it was so." He tried to make amends but only made matters worse by proposing to the Duke of Beaufort that young Worcester should become his Lord-in-Waiting. The Duke declined. Greville says: "had he (Albert) not been infatuated with his own dignity, he would never have contemplated the possibility of a young man resigning his office of *aide de camp* to the Duke to go and wait upon him at his trumpery and tiresome Court."

The outlook of both Victoria and Albert was curiously middle-class. They had both of them the same dislike for the very poor as the respectable working-classes have for casual labourers and slum-dwellers. Thus, in the "hungry 40's", Victoria called the poor Chartists wanton and worthless men, and the failure of their rising was described by Albert as—"What a glorious day for England!" In the terrible year 1848 there were an unusual number of Court festivities. He made speeches, however, about "Capital and Labour" and their reciprocal duties. "Golden Words" Sir Theodore Martin calls them. Victoria liked the nice clean tidy poor—Highland peasants, for instance, to whom she could take red flannel petticoats and bibles. The others she did not approve of. They did not go to Church, and they knew nothing of Albert and cared less.

In 1847 Albert was honoured by being elected Chancellor of the University of Cambridge by a majority of 116 votes over the Earl of Powis. The minority was so large that he hesitated about accepting it, but finally did so and was installed in July of the following year. It would—and later on did—give him a chance of doing something to educate the English. The Poet Laureate, Wordsworth, wrote the ode for the installation, which ran:

> "Albert, in thy race we cherish
> A nation's strength that will not perish,
> While England's scepter'd line,
> True to the King of Kings is found;
> Like that wise ancestor of thine,
> Who threw the Saxon shield o'er Luther's life.
> When first above the yells of bigot strife
> The trumpet of the Living Word,
> Assumed a voice of deep portentous sound,
> From gladdened Elba, to startled Tiber found."

More "Golden Words"!

CHAPTER FIVE

"Narquois et rusé Louis de l'âge philosophique, le monarque de notre choix conduit dextrement sa barque sur une bone liquide."

Mémoires D'Outre-Tombe, CHATEAUBRIAND.

SHORTLY before Albert's apotheosis at Cambridge, the European chancellories had been greatly agitated by an affair in which another member of his family played the *rôle* of *jeune premier.* It concerned the marriage of the young Queen Isabella of Spain. Her country had for some time been making itself a nuisance, but for the moment it happened to be fairly peaceful. Her Majesty being not yet quite sixteen, Queen Christina—her mother—was acting as Regent. As usual in such cases the question as to who should have the doubtful privilege of sharing the Royal Bed was being eagerly—not to say avidly—discussed. One might perhaps think that the decision was not of immediate urgency, considering her age; but her Ministers were not of that opinion. "The Southern temperament is ardent," said they. "What a disaster if the heir should arrive before the husband!" There were various applicants for the vacant position, including Isabella's cousin, the Duke of Cadiz, and Prince Leopold of Saxe-Coburg, a first cousin of Victoria's and Albert's; and in the background lurked Louis Philippe of France.

Louis had a pretty little plan of his own, which he considered would solve the question nicely. It was an open secret that the dissipated—and not quite normal—scion of the Spanish Royal House, the Duke of Cadiz, was *incapable*. Why not marry him to Isabella, at the same time bestowing his *own* son, le Duc de Montpensier, on her sister, the Infanta Fernanda, on whose children the succession would of necessity devolve? Why not indeed? Louis was quite aware of the instability of his throne and naturally wanted to strengthen his position. Had Victoria married le Duc de Nemours, all would have been so different. One feels very much inclined to wish that she had. Perhaps the moral character of the young man was less admirable than that of Albert, but how much more agreeable a country to live in would England have been, had it come under French, instead of German, influences! The French understand the art of living as no other people understand it, and, say what you will of them, they are not, and never have been, either moral prigs or kill-joys.

Whoever Isabella *did* marry, however, Louis was quite determined that it should not be a Coburg. European statesmen were not unaware of Stockmar's ambition to see a united Germany and of his stranglehold on Albert, and none of them wished to see that ambition realized: Louis least of all. The French hated their neighbours with more than the usual neighbourly hatred, and Louis sensed the danger to France which might eventuate if those frugal hard-working people, who increased and multiplied like rabbits, were to become a united country under the

Prussians whose trade since the dark ages had been war. Then, too, the Coburgs were spreading far too much. What with Leopold in Belgium, Albert in England, and another of them acting as husband in Portugal—to say nothing of who were filling minor jobs—they were really becoming as bad as the plague of Locusts Jehovah inflicted on the Egyptians because Pharaoh would not let the Children of Israel go. In England, although the Germans were not liked, German influence, owing to the Court, was very strong. And where Germany is entrenched there is always anti-French propaganda. Certainly the Coburgs must not bring off another *coup*.

The matter had been thoroughly thrashed out between Louis and Victoria during the visit she and Albert paid to the French sovereign in 1843 at the Chateau d'Eu. Louis promised that he would not propose one of his sons for Isabella or for her sister the Infanta until the chances of the latter, or of one of her children, succeeding to the throne were removed by heirs being born to Isabella herself. Lord Aberdeen, who had accompanied the Royal couple to France, thereupon agreed on behalf of Victoria that England would not support that candidature of Prince Leopold but that, apart from one of Louis's sons, any young man agreeable to Spain would be acceptable to England.

Albert was extremely reluctant to see his cousin's chances vanishing into thin air. A Coburg in Spain would have been a most useful asset to the family, and, had the marriage taken place, Leopold would have been in a position to advance German interests very considerably. The Coburgs were a clannish lot, and gratitude for Albert's support would have caused young Leopold to treat the Memoranda with all due respect. Besides which he was a presentable youth. Isabella had seen him, and she liked him much better than any of the other suggested husbands. To those of us who have unpolitical minds and are not enough versed in statecraft to apprehend the terrible consequences liable to result if that mysterious bogey "the balance of power" is upset the whole affair seems rather childish. It suggests the infantile "If you won't lend me your ball you shan't play with my doll" attitude. Nations, however, are bad neighbours, and, now that racial antipathies have replaced religion as a just cause for mutual hatred, they are obliged, like Agag, to walk delicately. In spite of the "Gentlemen's agreement", neither party trusted the other. Louis, tricky as a monkey, himself, was convinced that the Coburgs would do a bit of double-dealing if they got the chance, and, knowing Victoria's strong German sympathies, suspected both her and Albert of secretly working for Prince Leopold. Louis's Prime Minister, Guizot, who understood England as well as a Frenchman ever understands it, wrote: *"Le Gouvernment Anglais ne travaille pas positivement à ce mariage, mais il ne travaille pas non pluus efficacement a l'empêcher."* Precisely—the English Government had given its word not to *support* Leopold, but that did not engage it to work actively against him. If Isabella insisted on choosing him, so much the better. But Louis need not have feared trickery. Even Stockmar, who, like Albert, ardently desired the marriage, had decided that it must not be pressed in face of the French opposition.

Little more was heard of the matter until the autumn of 1846, when Louis calmly announced to a startled Europe that Isabella was to marry her cousin, the Duke of Cadiz, and that on the same day her sister was to take to herself le Duc de Montpensier! He had his excuse all ready. *Si trova tanti scusi*, as the Italians say! A hasty and highly indiscreet despatch of Palmerston's (not submitted to the Queen and only glanced at by Lord John Russell, the Prime Minister), served his purpose. In it Palmerston had criticized in rather strong language the incompetence of the Spanish government and urged it to press on Isabella the necessity of at once taking a husband, mentioning—among those suggested—Prince Leopold. The contents of the dispatch were communicated to Guizot, and the wily Louis pounced on the opportunity. The very name of Leopold was enough to his mind to prove that England had broken her promise not to support him. It is quite possible that he believed it, but he did not risk seeking an explanation. The matter was made worse by the letter Queen Marie Amélie wrote to Victoria announcing the marriage as if it were a matter of course and asking for her congratulations for her son, Duc de Montpensier! Albert was furious. Nothing can have been more faithless than the whole course of the French policy. We have been led on and triumphed over in the dark—a pitiful triumph to have deceived a friend, almost an only one, and at the very moment when he was making a sacrifice to friendship. *For the poor Queens clung to Leopold almost to the last.* Now he (Louis) explains that he was released from his word because Leopold was proposed contrary to Aberdeen's assurance. A fine invention! The Proverb is true *"Ehrlich wahrt am langesten"*. Less than two years after, the Orleans family were flying from France, and Louis and his family were fugitives in England. Thrones were quaking in 1848. Even England had its troubles, and so Victoria, with that real goodness of heart she always displayed in times of stress, forgave Louis and could not do enough for his Queen. She wrote: "That the Duchess of Montpensier, about whom we have been quarrelling for the last year and a half, should be here as a fugitive and dressed in the clothes I sent her and should come to thank *me* for *my* kindness, is a reverse of fortune which no novelist could devise and upon which one could moralize for ever." "Nothing," says Greville, "but the extraordinary good sense of Prince Albert, with the boundless influence he has over her, keeps her affectionate feelings under due restraint." Albert was too righteous a man to forgive so easily. "The worship of truth and reason becomes every day more and more a matter of conscience with me," he wrote to Stockmar.

During all these agitations Albert and Stockmar never for a moment lost sight of their pet scheme, the unification of Germany under Prussia. "I am deep in German politics with Charles (Prince Charles of Leiningen) who understands them *au fond*," he writes to Stockmar from Scotland,

"and we write memorandums with a view to strengthening German unity by means of a living union, and keep pounding away at Austria as the main obstruction. I maintain that England's true position is to be the defence and support of States whose independent development is sought to be impeded from without." It is interesting to note how well Stockmar's pupil had learnt his lesson. He then proceeded to draw up a scheme for German unity, regardless of the fact that, as Consort of the Queen of England, it was no business of his. The last paragraph of it is significant in the light of after events. *"My own view is that the political reformation of Germany lies entirely in the hands of Prussia, and that Prussia has only to will to accomplish this event."* He goes on to say that if Prussia would only adopt *his* recommendations she would become one of the most important European powers. In 1849 Greville in a letter to Henry Reeve wrote: "Aberdeen talked to me about the Prince with many ecomiums; he said his only fault was his excessive Germanism, and his being such a vehement and uncompromising partisan of the German Imperial Unity scheme, and abettor of Prussian dangers." Aberdeen had told Greville that Albert's views were generally sound and wise, but that "He goes all lengths with Prussia and will not hear of a moderate plan—a species of Federalism, based on the treaty of Vienna and the old relations of Germany—and insists on a new German Empire with Prussia at its head."

Stockmar tried to hold him back, considering, very sensibly, that he had left Germany when he was too young to understand properly the conditions prevailing there. He knew that it was no use trying to rush matters, but Albert —German to the core—was ready, as Lord Aberdeen had seen, to go to all lengths. Greatly daring—"when the cat was away"—he drew up a memorandum embodying at full—very full—length his suggestions for German unity and sent it to the Courts of Austria, Prussia and Saxony. He met with but little encouragement, and when the "cat came back" it showed its claws. Stockmar's plan for the regeneration of the Fatherland was not the same as Albert's, besides which it was not the moment to stir up any more political passions; they were raging violently enough already. Hungary was in revolt against Austria, and Austria against itself; Paris had had another taste of revolution and a day of barricades; and the Diet, through Prussia, had attacked Denmark on the ground that Holstein belonged to the Germanic Confederation: the first of the wars caused by this highly complicated question. The hopes that Albert had in the National Assembly at Frankfort were disappointed. None of the various schemes for a new German Constitution materialized. It was, for the time being, the end of what the Duke of Coburg, Albert's brother, called "the Frankfort Dream". Poor Albert wrote sadly: "The world is worse than ever!" But the seed had been well sown, and, though Albert and Stockmar were not to see the promised land, their efforts, still not to be relaxed, had done much to bring about its future realization.

Naturally enough all these activities on behalf of Germany did not tend to make Albert any more popular with Her Majesty's Ministers. They resented, too, his and Stockmar's constant interference in State matters and considered it definitely bad policy of the Queen to allow it. Palmerston—his *bête noire*—treated him with almost exaggerated indifference, pointedly ignoring his wishes and taking momentous decisions without consulting either him or Victoria. Albert, for his part, did not hesitate to show the contempt he felt for the English nobility; their gambling, their drinking, their passion for sport and their lack of interest in intellectual pursuits. He considered them in many ways little better than barbarians; at the same time he envied them their easy manners and social charm. They returned the contempt of this "German nobody" with interest, treating him with cold polite indifference. It was all very unfortunate. He who is apparently without human weaknesses is always distrusted and suspected—and rightly so; and if he happens to be a foreigner the dice are loaded against him. Moreover, Albert's close association with Stockmar made matters worse. It was said in the Palace that if he were wanted he was always to be found in Stockmar's room. He had everything to gain by making himself liked by the English aristocracy, and yet he seems to have gone out of his way to antagonize them.

Victoria could never see that he fell short of perfection in any degree. She was in many ways a very simple woman, and yet she had her feet planted far more firmly on the ground than ever he had. She was naturally inclined to take life as she found it, so she did not suffer the constant disillusionments and disappointments *he* experienced through the wicked perversity of his fellow creatures. Their failure to appreciate her "dear Lord" aroused her indignation much more easily than did any of their human shortcomings. How she loved the precious months when she had him all to herself at Balmoral! To the end of his life her heart beat like that of a young girl at the sight of her Albert in his kilts. One may, perhaps, be permitted a smile at those naïve entries in "Leaves from our Journal in the Highlands", but some of them are strangely pathetic, almost tragic, for there is always tragedy in a love so great that all the light of a human life is centred in it. Albert was never in love with his wife in this sense—great love is always one-sided—and that she never guessed it nor for a moment lost her utter confidence in him constitutes his greatest claim to distinction.

They had much in common. Their complete lack of any sense of humour was a strong bond; there is nothing so fatal to married happiness as that one of the partners should possess it and not the other. Travelling with a child, said Victoria, reminded her of her own childhood; and Albert replied that "Parents lived their lives over again in their children". "The chief beauty of mountain scenery consisted in its constant changes," he discovered; while she rejoiced that her "dear Prince", who had seen so much, admired Edinburgh. Scotland, he thought, was not unlike Germany. Dalkeith, blessed among towns, looked *very* German! Higher praise he could not bestow. She accompanied him when he went deer-stalking, frequently keeping as near as she could to the guns; and how proud she was when he made a kill! Caledonia might be wild, but it was not stern to these poetic children. They revelled in the grey mist-enshrouded Highland landscape, and, when in the long Scotch twilight they sat together in their hideous dining-room with its tartan carpets and Landseer pictures listening to the even more hideous catterwaulings of the bagpipes, life—at least to Victoria —seemed very sweet.

Education was a fetish with Albert. He saw in himself its admirable results and frankly deplored what he considered the lack of it in England. He would have agreed with the famous Frenchman who, while having—unlike most of his fellow-countrymen—a whole-hearted admiration for the English, considered them the worst educated people in Europe. What exactly *does* constitute a good education? It is futile to dogmatize, but some people still think that the mental discipline, knowledge of the humanities and historical perspective—among other things—which the thorough classical education given up to recent times at the public schools and universities afforded to those who chose to profit by it, turned out men who were very well educated indeed—men such as Gladstone, Manning, Palmerston, Macaulay, Tennyson, who are hard to find nowadays. If, however, the greatest good of the greatest number and a general level of mediocrity is the highest educational aim to be sought, then the classics—like dignity, leisure, religion and many other beautiful things—must be thrown overboard. Albert was essentially a modernist; he was born a hundred years too soon. Hence, to a great extent, his unhappiness. He was like a fish out of water in the aristocratic society of the first half of the Victorian period—a society which was still largely eighteenth century in its outlook. He had no use for a classical education, and, taking advantage of his position as Chancellor of Cambridge, he drew up, in collaboration with Dr. Whewell, a new scheme of studies, including practical and scientific subjects with courses of lectures—attendance being compulsory. This was, for good or ill, the beginning of the modern system of education and the death knell of the scholar. The classics, like the Gods of Valhalla, will soon be but twilight ghosts. Most of the young people of to-day despise not only the great Greek and Roman literature but also their own.

Perhaps Albert was never so happy in England as he was when planning the Great Exhibition of 1851. It was his own idea, his aim being to assemble under the same roof the art and commerce of the entire civilized world so that nations might meet nations in brotherly love and compare progress. The scheme was coldly received by the public. Albert summoned a public meeting to invite subscriptions, and it was at this public meeting that Bishop Samuel Wilberforce coined the now historic phrase "the dignity of labour". Money was slow to come in. *Punch* published a cartoon by Leech representing Albert cap in hand begging with the parody beneath:

"Pity the sorrows of a poor young Prince,
Whose costly schemes have borne him to your door;
Who's in a fix, the matter not to mince,
Oh! help him out, and commerce swell your store!"

Little by little the expenses were guaranteed—chiefly

by leading business firms and manufacturers—and, as Paxton's appalling structure drew to completion, Albert's heart swelled with pride and joy. Victoria rejoiced with him. "My dearest Prince is, as usual, full of occupations. . . . I always stand amazed at his wonderful mind; *such* large views of everything. He is *very, very* great. And then there is always such a desire to do everything without shining himself, but he *does* shine."

Contrary to popular expectation it was a triumphant success financially. It undoubtedly stimulated international commerce, but whether it was an unmixed blessing is an open question. Foreign nations gained far more through studying English methods than England gained by a knowledge of theirs. Then, too, it gave an immense impetus to the gross materialism which was the curse of the late nineteenth century and which is causing the bankruptcy of modern civilization. It also began the craze for advertisement and the curious love of the masses for seeing everything *en gros*. Walls of tinned fruit, miles of motor-cars, pyramids of apples—a craze which is a veritable obsession with the great American public.

Curiously enough the Exhibition did not arouse the enthusiasm of Albert's great admirer, Lady Lyttelton, who writes in 1851 to the Hon. Coraline Lyttelton: "Your treatise on the Exhibition is very good, and I agree that so far I have *no* enthusiasm about the trade and industry part of it, and think that passage in Prince Albert's speech a mere piece of German philosophy, worthless at best." She is glad that it has given employment to so many poor workmen and admires the good feeling of the thousands present at the opening—"who had such a mass of mischief in their power and who were fully expected to use it". She says the great undertaking must redound to Albert's honour —"everywhere except in London", and "show what he is made of, as to talent at least." She goes on to say: "I believe it is quite universally sneered at and abominated by the *beau monde* and will only increase the contempt for the Prince among the fine folk. But so would anything he does."

It was during the preparations for the Exhibition that Peel died—sincerely regretted by the whole nation. He was, perhaps, the only statesman with whom Albert was on terms of real friendship and with whose aims he sympathized. Peel, he felt—like he himself—acted always from the highest motives—*so* unlike Palmerston, whom they both hated cordially. Who was there now to restrain that odious obstinate old person?

CHAPTER SIX

"For some must watch while some must sleep.
So runs the world away."
SHAKESPEARE (*Hamlet*)

THE Great Exhibition was over; the "Captains and the Kings" departed, and—"lest we forget"—the preposterous structure removed to the slopes of Sydenham. "Hush," said Max Beerbohm, drawing down the blinds of the railway-carriage in which he was journeying to Brighton, "we shall soon be passing the Crystal Palace." Albèrt had thoroughly enjoyed the whole business; it was his *magnum opus*, and, now that it was over, he missed the stir and bustle and the pleasure he had felt in showing his achievement to Royal visitors. He missed Peel, too. Palmerston was being more tiresome than ever. With jaunty grace he lightly brushed aside all opposition: he was the servant of the nation, not of Albert. When invited to Buckingham Palace to explain his naughty ways, he protested, with crocodile tears in his eyes and his tongue in his cheek, that "never, never" had he failed, nor was he capable of failing, in respect to Her Majesty; but he continued in his evil courses.

The visit to London of the notorious Austrian, General Hagnau, caused a serious breach. The General had been employed to put down rebellion in Hungary and had done it with peculiar bestiality and brutality; flogging women, among other things. The most attractive manifestation of the genius of England, he considered, was its bitter beer, so he hastened to inspect Barclay and Perkins' Brewery. He was a tall sinister-looking person with enormous flowing moustaches, and, as his face was familiar owing to the numerous caricatures which had appeared in the papers, he was at once recognized and mobbed, escaping considerably damaged through a side entrance. The Austrian Government demanded an apology, and Palmerston wrote one in which, while regretting the circumstance, he suggested that "General Hyena", as he was called, had better have kept out of the way, considering his evil reputation. He showed his answer to Victoria and Albert and to Lord John Russell. They highly disapproved of the qualifying passage and were furious when Palmerston told them it had already been sent to the Ambassador—who was even more furious. They insisted on his withdrawing the note, whereupon he threatened to resign. "Now thank we all our God!" sang the delighted Albert. And then, to his intense disgust, Palmerston submitted and altered the offending document! It must not be thought that Albert for a moment approved of General Hagnau's methods, but he disapproved far more of any affront to a foreign country. Ambassadors were sacrosanct beings, and the masses must learn to submit themselves lowly and reverently towards their betters—even when their "betters" were worse than "betters" had any right to be! "We in London," said Albert, "have, in the

Hagnau demonstration, had a slight foretaste of what an unregulated mass of illiterate people is capable."

Palmerston was not the only Minister who disliked Albert's constant interference in matters which it was customary to leave in the hands of the Cabinet. Lord Clarendon said in 1854: "The Queen and Prince Albert interfere and meddle in a very inconvenient manner with everything they can." Albert, however, had a profound contempt for Parliament as well as a very exalted idea of what should be the privileges of monarchs. Stockmar, in a memorandum written in 1850, urged him to influence the Queen to exercise more effectively the Royal Prerogative. "The Sovereign," said he, "should be in the position of a permanent premier. . . . It would be unreasonable that a King as able as any of his Ministers should be prevented from making use of such qualities as he possessed at ministerial councils." He also said that he must lose no opportunity of asserting the power of the throne, lest the people should eventually come to regard the monarch as a mere figurehead. Albert agreed with him. William III had presided over his own Council; and, in a speech at the hundred and fiftieth anniversary of the Society for the Propagation of the Gospel in Foreign Parts, he (Albert) made the amazing statement that "William III was the greatest monarch the country had to boast of"! Fortunately they had Palmerston to contend with, and Victoria's strong common sense led her to prefer constitutional methods of government.

Albert's health was steadily growing more and more

unsatisfactory. He took very little exercise, and he began to grow fat and puffy. He slept badly, and his stomach behaved worse than ever. In vain did he drink hot water and purge himself. After the death of Peel, Victoria wrote to Stockmar, who, with his usual rudeness, had left without saying good-bye to take the air at Coburg (as ever, "Master of himself"!): "You do not answer my anxious letter. Pray *do* listen to our *Entreaties* to come. It will do you good to be with my *Beloved Prince*. He *longs* for you. Since the night of your poor friend's (Peel) death he again wakes so easily, and this is a sad distress to me. Clark admits that it is the mind. Diet has been of no avail." One fancies that Victoria did not often undergo the experience of finding her letters unanswered.

But, ill or well, nothing could stop Albert's devastating passion for trying to run the world. "It was a gigantic task," said the Saxe-Coburg Minister, Count Vizhun, "for a German Prince to think and act for all these millions of British subjects." It was indeed; and it had been better for all had he left it alone. Not a single dispatch was sent from the Foreign Office which he did not see and, if he thought necessary, alter. Not a report of any ambassador was kept from him. And he received every day bundles of papers from all the other State departments. Besides all this he kept up a regular correspondence with his German relations and with other European Royalties—to say nothing of British Ambassadors and the Governors of Colonies. And a letter from Albert was no "scrap of paper"! A never-ending flood of memoranda poured forth from his untiring pen; those he wrote on Oriental questions alone between 1853 and 1857 amounted to fifty folio volumes. Writing to Stockmar in 1854, he said: "I have just worked out a plan for the reorganizing of the army in the Crimea. I have just completed a memorandum on Examinations and New Rules of Admission for the Diplomatic Body. I am now engaged in preparing an address on the influence of Science and Art on our Manufacturers."

In addition to these activities he lost no opportunity of speaking in public. From the Society for the Propagation of the Gospel he skipped lightly to the Cattle Show, sandwiching in between advice to artists at the Royal Academy dinner. Then there was the Society for improving the condition of Domestic Servants and teaching them thrift. It was addressed by the Archbishop of Canterbury, the Bishop of London, "Soapy Sam", Cardinal Manning, the Prime Minister and Albert himself. Albert afterwards received a letter of appreciation from "Your Royal Highness's young humble servant, C.A.A. A servant of good character." It does not seem to have occurred to any of these distinguished gentlemen that the wages then paid to servants were a disgrace to a so-called civilized country, as also were their working hours, and that their condition in many cases was not far removed from slavery. One must, however, give Albert full credit for his broadminded idea about the reform of the public-house. He advocated cafés similar to those so universal abroad, where people could order anything they wanted and sit in pleasant surroundings listening to music or playing games. There were rumours that Albert did not write his own speeches, that they were too well written to have been composed by a German; and there is no doubt that they were always—at least, at the beginning of his public career—submitted to Stockmar; but it seems difficult when reading them to imagine that they can have been written by anyone else. They are so portentously dull. The *Spectator* said: "There is an individuality about them which stamps their real authorship" and went on to say that if they were not his own "the Prince must be endowed with the facility of delivering other men's ideas in a spontaneous fashion". He was; and he was also so thoroughly impregnated with Stockmar's ideas that the Stockmar idiom had become second nature to him. Stockmar—cool, calm and capable—smiled to himself as he directed the activities of his model pupil.

The success of the Exhibition had considerably raised Albert's *prestige* in the country, and he was to have yet another triumph—nothing less than the dismissal of his arch-enemy Palmerston! With his usual impetuosity the popular Foreign Minister had assured the French Ambassador that the English Government entirely approved of Louis Napoleon's *coup d'état*, and, as usual, he had consulted neither the Prime Minister nor the Queen nor—*bien entendu!*—Albert. This was too much even for Lord John Russell. He requested Palmerston's resignation; and Lord Granville, a *protégé* of Albert, was appointed Foreign Secretary. His triumph was short-lived, for, a few months later, Lord John's Government was defeated. Then came the brief Ministry of Lord Derby, followed by a Coalition with Lord Ab -deen as Prime Minister and Gladstone as Chancellor of the Exchequer. Palmerston returned to the Cabinet—though not to the Foreign Office—to the great joy of the people, who loved and understood this breezy pleasant-mannered typically English aristocrat.

The Great Exhibition—which Albert hoped would cause nations to forget animosities, beat their words into ploughshares and unite in friendly commercial rivalry—did not fulfil its purpose. Mankind remained as perverse as ever. Well might he exclaim, "When I speak unto them of peace they make them ready for war," for the dogs of war were again loosed. The story of the Crimean Campaign is, of course, familiar to all. Russia wanted Turkey, and religion came once more to the aid of strife—the French demanding the Holy Sepulchre for the Roman Church, and the Russians claiming it for that of Greece. If to-day one asks: "And why did we meddle?" one must again quote the Italian saying, *Si trova tanti scusi!* There was that delicate nursling, the balance of power; one could not let Russia have command of the Archipelago. In the last War it was "poor little Belgium" and the "scrap of paper", and in the next it will be Heaven knows what; but it will be *something*. Better destroy the results of a hundred years of civilization and millions of young lives than give up one *iota* of our national pretensions, say the old gentlemen who guide our destinies.

All the old tricks to arouse popular enthusiasm were

resorted to. All the old catchwords which convince the young and simple that God wants them to go and be killed were brought into action; "National Honour," "Our Gallant Allies," "We'll Bait the Russian Bear," "We don't want to fight, but by Jingo if we do!"

> "We've got the men, we've got the guns,
> We've got the money too . . ."

and so on.

In the last War the Russian Bear—benevolent this time —turned into a steam-roller which was to crush the Germans until they were consumed. But doubtless the same methods were used with the Children of Israel by the prophets of Baal, when Ahab went up to fall at Ramoth Gilead.

During all this war agitation the strong undercurrent of hostility towards Albert and Stockmar, which had long been waiting an occasion to manifest itself, burst into full flood. Albert was a foreigner, a German. He did not ride, shake hands or dress like an Englishman—"Just look at the cut of his clothes!" Then, too, he neither betted nor gambled and took no interest in women. And Stockmar —surely an adventurer and a spy—was his bosom friend and adviser: some said, his master. He was the cunning agent of Russia and was in the pay of the Emperor. Once, when he had not left Coburg for six months, he was reported to be hidden at Buckingham Palace plotting with Albert. When Palmerston resigned owing to a difference with the Prime Minister, it was because he had discovered that Albert was a traitor and was betraying State secrets to foreign powers! And when Palmerston withdrew his resignation, everyone was delirious with joy. There were even rumours that Albert had been committed to the Tower, and thousands waited to see his entry. In another country he would have fared badly: in another century he would have been beheaded.

As a matter of fact, he was quite innocent, though he had only himself to blame for his unpopularity; he had never tried to be English. The chief thing against him was that he had worked hard for peace in a country stricken with war fever. "Here the rage for war," he says, "has reached a pitch that I should hardly have thought possible. The public has kindly made me the scapegoat *for the war not having begun.* It is said that the Emperor rules England from Russia, that I whisper into Victoria's ear and the voice of the only *British* Minister, Palmerston, is not listened to but, instead, he has been intrigued out of Court and Cabinet! The stupidest trash is babbled to the public, so stupid that —as they say in Coburg—you would not give it to the pigs for litter." So great was the tumult that in January 1854 Lord Aberdeen and Lord John Russell spoke in both Houses of Parliament in Albert's defence. They made it clear that Albert could not be a mere cipher; that he was actually a Privy Councillor and Victoria's natural adviser, and the Ministers vouched for his loyalty. The mutterings died down, though he never became popular.

Well, they had their war; and, as usual, when the first excitement subsided and the appalling sufferings of the troops, due to the criminal unpreparedness of the hospital arrangements, became public knowledge, they wished they hadn't had it. For it was not the walk-over that the politicians had promised. Wars never are.

There was a curious rumour about the death of the Emperor Nicholas. It was said that when the news of the fall of Sebastopol came he was in bed with a cold. His despair and anger were so great that he sent for his doctor and asked him to give him a poison that would kill a man with little pain in four days. At first Dr. Marx refused to do so; but you cannot say "No" to an autocrat, and he had to comply with the request: Nicholas took the dose. On the third day his daughter, who was nursing him, suspected that something was wrong and, on tasting the medicine, guessed the truth. Towards evening, when she saw that her father was dying, she opened all the doors and screamed out: "The Emperor is poisoned; send for Dr. Marx." The doctor came and told his story. "He can't live through the night," he said. Nicholas died in a few hours, and the doctor went home and cut his throat.

Albert's beloved Prussia had behaved very badly during the war. Frederick William was afraid to quarrel with his brother-in-law, Nicholas. He admired and feared him and, above all, envied him. He would have loved to be an autocrat himself, but it didn't run to it. His Ambassador in London, the industrious Bunsen, was recalled on account of his anti-Russian sympathies. Bunsen had worked out five different schemes for the regeneration of his country, each one on a different principle and worked out to the last detail!

"Prussia, unhappy country!" wrote Albert. "The King is the tool of Russian dictation, partly from fear of Russia, partly from an absurdly sentimental feeling for the Emperor as representative of the Holy Alliance." He was highly indignant at what he called the *unverstand* of the King of Prussia whose war policy had exhibited all the dishonesty, unreliability and low cunning one usually associates with Prussian diplomacy. But Albert, when smitten on *one* cheek by Prussia, was not content with turning the other to the smiter—*Il lui presentait aussi le derrière!* Notwithstanding Frederick William's despicable conduct, his German soul was enchanted at the suggestion of a marriage between his favourite daughter, the Princess Royal, and the Crown Prince of Prussia.[1] The Prince was an estimable young man, but he was a German; and England had every reason for turning the coldest of shoulders towards Germany. As was only to be expected, the news of the match was received with intense resentment, partly on account of Albert's German proclivities, and partly on account of Prussia's contemptible attitude during the war. *The Times* called the Hohenzollern "a paltry German dynasty". It gave a tremendous impetus to the onward march of those Christian soldiers under the "good old German God" to their ideal *"Welt Politik"*! English *prestige*, English power, English money, were entirely at their service, and they made full use of their opportunities.

There is little doubt that, had it not been for the wholehearted German sympathies of the Court, Prussia's

---

[1]Nephew of the childless king.

ambitions would have been seriously checked. Palmerston loathed Germany and all its works. When Prussia tried to dominate the German Federation, the King wrote to Victoria asking for her support and encouragement. Palmerston, hearing of the letter from Bunsen, told her that she must not correspond with foreign royalties except on purely personal matters. With the aid of the reluctant Albert he drafted a reply and insisted on her copying it and sending to the King. As Albert in private letters to him had repeatedly urged him to assert Prussian power, it put both him and Victoria in a very difficult position. A similar incident had occurred during the Portuguese troubles in 1847. The Queen had written to ask for Victoria's support against threatened revolution; but Palmerston treated the dispute as a Coburg family affair due to the machinations of a German confidant of the Queen's husband, a man named Dietz, who had tried to be the Stockmar of Portugal. Palmerston again dictated a letter, which Victoria had to send, full of warnings against Dietz and strongly recommending his dismissal. Oh, for some faithful henchman to deal with him as the servants of Henry the Second dealt with Becket! But no bolt from the blue came to their aid. In 1855 they had the mortification of seeing their arch-enemy Prime Minister; and he remained in office for ten years.

With regard to Albert's ambitions for Prussia the Crown Prince of Germany wrote in 1870: "I cannot help myself at this crisis from thinking a great deal of the plans of my late father-in-law (the Prince Consort)—as also the

late King (Leo I) of the Belgians in conjunction with old
Baron Stockmar—entertained for a united Germany under
a monarchial head.   God willed that these men should
conceive the notion of a free German Imperial State that
in the true sense of the word should march at the forefront
of civilization and be in a position to develop and bring to
bear all noble ideals of the modern world, so that *through
German influence the rest of the world should be humanized
and people diverted from those frivolous French tendencies."*
Well, well—"A light to lighten the Gentiles"!

Had Albert and Victoria had the same sympathy with
Italy in her struggle for freedom as they had for German
ambitions, that freedom might have been attained much
sooner and a great deal of war and misery averted.   But
neither of them lifted a finger to help.   Indeed, they viewed
with intense dismay the weakening of the idea of royalty
implied in Italy's struggle against the hateful tyranny of
Austria, and with this dismay they associated the fate of all
the petty rulers who would certainly lose their jobs were
the cause of liberty to triumph.   And yet they professed
profound indignation at France insisting on the cession of
Savoy in return for the benevolent—and grudging—
neutrality she observed.   Both of them detested the King
of Sardinia and stood for the *status quo* and Austrian
brutality.   "With regard to Sardinia," wrote Victoria
inspired by her dear Prince, "if she provokes hostilities
unjustly and places herself in the wrong, she will get no
support from *me*."   She didn't get it in any case, but, apart
from the Court, the sympathies of England were entirely

with Italy in her long travail and in the end had great influence in bringing about a united Italy.

The Crimean War, the acute consciousness of the hostility felt towards him and his overwork and bad health had aged Albert terribly. And after 1857 Stockmar came no more to England. The most frantic appeals to return left him unmoved. He wrote to Albert: "In the spring of 1837, now twenty years ago, I returned to England to give what help I could to Princess Victoria, now Queen. This year I shall be seventy and am no longer equal, mentally or physically, to perform the laborious and exhausting office of a paternal friend and trusted confessor." They were to meet again twice: in 1859, when Albert visited Coburg and Stockmar dined with him; and in the following year, when he and Victoria went there to see their son-in-law and their daughter who had just given birth to a little son whom, had they been able to foresee the future, they would surely have strangled immediately!

After the Crimean War England settled down into the smug prosperous respectability known as "Victorianism". Before the Great War it was the fashion to deride it. "How Victorian!" we said of women who neither smoked, drank nor swore and who were quaint enough to go to church. Now, however, the pendulum is swinging in the other direction, and "Victorianism" is quite fashionable among the "best people". We no longer sneer at it; indeed, in these lean times we are inclined to envy the Victorians their peace and plenty. They were a curious mixture of genuine piety, simplicity and hypocrisy, and they were hag-ridden by the

Nonconformist conscience. Human nature, we are told, never changes in its essentials; but its varieties are infinite, and human beings can seem strangely unlike each other when living under totally different conditions. To call a spade a spade was the height of vulgarity; it was simply "not done". Women had no legs; they possessed limbs. False modesty caused the w.c. to be regarded as a disgraceful secret and spoken of in a shocked whisper. All those of us who are over fifty must remember being drawn furtively aside by our host when visiting and being shown the where-abouts of the accursed thing. Nowadays it is pointed out with pride. It has assumed almost the importance of a family seat—especially in fiction! Having a baby was even worse;

> "God moves in a mysterious way,
> His wonders to perform,"

sang Cowper. "Surely we cannot do less," said the Victorian ladies.

It was an ugly age; perhaps no civilization has ever devoted .itself with such enthusiasm to the *culte* of the hideous. Architecture reached its lowest ebb. Art became photographic, and a picture must either tell a pretty story or depict a pretty landscape; a sunset for choice. The lovely Queen Anne, Chippendale and Hepplewhite furniture was relegated to the attics and replaced by solid mahogany "suites" or gimcrack painted rubbish—black papier mâché and the like. Antimacassars adorned the backs of chairs and the plush-covered sofas of strange distorted shapes. On the mantelpieces, with their scalloped and tasselled draperies, were wax flowers with glass covers, lustres and vases of fell design, while "occasional" tables, made to knock over on every occasion, exhibited beadwork boxes and photographic albums. Wallpapers and carpets of appalling patterns completed the scheme of interior decoration. It is inexplicable that nearly three hundred years of beautiful architecture, furniture, silver, glass, pictures and panelling should have been followed by such an orgy of ugliness.

The Court showed to the full the prevailing bad taste; the private apartments of the royal palaces were a nightmare. The coach Albert designed for the funeral of the Duke of Wellington was worthy of the Chamber of Horrors, and the "Albert Memorial" has made us a byword among nations. We never have produced any sculptors of genius, and those of the nineteenth century are an awful reminder of the depths that can be plumbed by the incompetent. But we must not forget that, by a curious paradox, Albert was the first to collect Italian primitives. Some of the best pictures in the Royal Collection were chosen by him. And, if it was not an age of good taste, it certainly produced— at all events in literature and politics—men of a very different calibre from those of our own day.

Though we have shed Victorian hypocrisy, its influence still lingers blighting the pleasant land of England. Cromwell's legacy, put out to interest by Victoria, has given us *Dora*. In place of the sanctimonious Roundheads who suppressed the freedom and happiness of rural life—the games and the singing—we have meddling bureaucrats, inspectors and inquisitors, poking their noses into our homes and, with a tyranny only to be found in a so-called free country, telling us when we may eat, drink and buy the necessities of life; what we may do, and when we may do it. And the people will it so.

And yet, after all, a lingering fragrance clings to our memories of Victorian days—"the tender grace of a day that is dead"; Mayfair and St. James's on a spring morning, with their Georgian dignity and distinction still unimpaired; the jingling of the smart hansoms; the intensely feminine girls; the jolly free-and-easy music-halls; the old shops and the unhurried life. Even the dull Sundays: not so dull, either, to the Londoner with plenty of friends or to the country lover. Ah, we were young then! Perhaps our children "forty years on" will feel the same about to-day.

CHAPTER SEVEN

ALBERT did not allow ill-health and worry to interfere with his appalling industry. On the contrary he worked harder than ever. Even when there was no political crisis on hand to give him the chance of writing a lengthy memorandum, he was at his desk at seven and insisted on poor Victoria also rising at that ungodly hour. The excellent woman was intensely grateful to him for teaching her to practise the precept, "Early to bed and early to rise"! And yet she might well have been allowed to sleep an hour or so longer. She was Queen—and no mere figurehead. She took an active part in affairs of State, and babies arrived with disconcerting regularity. By nine o'clock Albert had read all the papers and made a *précis* of the important news for his wife. Then they went for a short walk, he walking very fast and she trotting breathlessly after him. When he felt it was his duty to take part in a shoot, he would never stay out more than two hours. He could not, he said, understand how anyone could make shooting or hunting the business of the day. That it would hardly be worth while to undertake the expense and trouble of organizing a shoot or a hunt for less than a day did not occur to his unsportsmanlike mind. Even in the country he "never relaxed". There were his model farms to run, the grounds at Osborne to be laid out, his system of converting sewage into manure to be tried. Tried it was, but unfortunately it did not prove any more successful than were the moral frescoes painted at the House of Commons under his expert directions and which, like so much early piety, faded completely away with the passing of their youth! Then, too, he supervised the education of the labourers in the Royal Estates, from whom he exacted a high standard of moral character.

He was at his best when alone with his family; indeed, family life helped him to forget his unpopularity in the outside world. He was a kind affectionate father though a stern disciplinarian, as were most fathers in those days. But he never understood children. He did not see that "Bertie's" charming disposition, his quick intelligence and intuitive understanding and sympathy were infinitely more valuable qualities than his own dreary ability to assimilate facts: and so they were always strangers to each other. His sons regarded him with dutiful affection and respectful awe, but he was never given the freedom of that most delightful of secret dwelling-places—the loving trusting heart of a boy. That was his tragedy, for there was no question of his affection for them. He could not, however, leave them alone for a moment, fussing over every detail of their education and supervising every hour of their leisure. Even when they were allowed to play with selected boys of good moral character, there was he in the midst of them to see that the games were such as he approved! Their natural boyish instincts were given no outlet, for, if they stood in awe of their father, they were frightened to death of their mother. Perhaps part of his anxiety for their moral welfare was due to his fear that they might develop some of the undesirable qualities of their grandfather, the Duke of Kent. Greville, speaking to Lord Melbourne about Victoria before she became Queen, said: "Everyone knows that her father was the greatest rascal that ever went unhung." It is infinitely to their credit that they all turned out so well. When in after years "Bertie" was called over the coals by Victoria for his misdeeds, he might well have sung: "I might have been much better if my father had been worse!"[1]

With his daughters he was more successful. Girls do not require the intensive education so desirable for an heir to a throne, and, curiously enough, his favourite daughter, the Princess Royal, liked being educated. She swallowed with avidity the heavy mental diet with which he delighted to feed her mind; literature, music, drainage, political economy; nothing came amiss to her. He even succeeded in teaching her his own lack of tact, for—Teutonic as were his educational ideas and his manner of imparting them— she was almost as unpopular in her adopted country, Germany, as he was in England. He missed her terribly after her marriage; she was the only member of his family with whom he could hold mental converse, for Victoria was in no way attracted by the things of the intellect.

Christmas 1860 was spent at Windsor—it was Albert, by the way, who introduced the charming German custom of the Christmas-tree into England—and the Princess was

---

[1]A. P. Herbert. "Derby Day."

the only absent member of the family. He wrote to her:
"We have missed you greatly at our Christmas table;

> Our dearest heads were counted o'er,
> A dearest one is here no more!

Oh, if only you with Fritz and the children were only
with us! Louis was an accession. He is a very good, dear
fellow, who pleases us better and better daily. . . . Prejudice
walking to and fro in flesh and blood is my horror, and
alas! a phenomenon so common, and people plume themselves so much on their prejudices as signs of decision of
character and greatness of mind, nay, of true patriotism,
and all the while they are simply the product of narrowness
of intellect and narrowness of heart."

"Louis"—Prince Louis of Hesse—was another prospective German addition to the family; he had recently become
engaged to the Princess Alice.

The letter, a real *cri de cœur*, throws a powerful light
on Albert's bitter resentment at the unrelenting hostility
he had experienced and at the same time shows how
singularly obtuse even the ultra-intelligent can be when it
is a question of their own prejudices. He simply could not
understand that his intimacy with Stockmar, his intense
preoccupation with German politics and affairs, and all these
German alliances, combined with his German accent and
appearance, could have only one result in so insular a
country as England. True, he had thrown himself eagerly
into every philanthropic scheme and spent himself untiringly
in trying to reform the barbaric islanders among whom Fate

had been unkind enough to cast his lot. But he had never for a moment tried to identify himself with their interests and amusements. The establishment of a racing-stable and two days a week hunting would have done more for him in a month than twenty years of solicitude for their moral welfare, for—regrettable though it is—we always dislike those who try to improve us. And, by a natural paradox, the popularity he would thus have acquired would have enormously increased his influence as a reformer of social abuses. "Bertie", who from his parents' point of view was so lamentable a failure, was a case in point. When he became King his lightest word had more effect than a hundred of his father's long dreary memoranda. Had he succeeded to the throne twenty years earlier we might have been spared the European War.

Albert took himself terribly seriously. He had, as we have seen, very little sense of humour and none of that slightly cynical good-humoured tolerance which is so striking an English characteristic. A joke lasted him a long time. Lady Bloomfield tells us that when she was in waiting the Queen one day expressed a wish to hear her sing. In fear and trembling she sang one of Grisi's famous airs but omitted the shake at the end. Her Majesty noticed the omission and, turning to Lady Normanby, said: "Does not your sister shake, Lady Normanby?" "Oh, yes, Ma'am," was the reply, *"she is shaking all over!"* Albert told this anecdote on every possible occasion for months afterwards, never failing to find in it the same zest. Like all dull people he loved practical jokes. If he saw anyone catch his foot in a mat and fall or sit on his hat accidentally, he would go into fits of laughter. His own jokes were thoroughly German in their heaviness. "My nephew is a dull boy," said the Duke of Cambridge. Perhaps those genial pleasant people who go through life "turning to mirth all things of earth", themselves included, are less worthy of admiration than are the more serious-minded, but they at least help to make the wheels of life go round. *La Cigale, qui, ayant chanté tout l'été*, found herself in so unfortunate a condition when winter arrived, was certainly a more agreeable neighbour than the tiresome industrious ant who was probably glad enough to ask her to dinner and who, one hopes, was called upon to contribute to her support! Albert would not have agreed with so deplorably immoral a theory. He admired those captains of industry who in tedious interviews tell us that their success is due to their always having risen at five o'clock in the morning and never having wasted a penny. And he himself did a good deal to popularize the importance of being earnest! The mid-Victorian period set a premium on portentous dullness. The newspapers devoted columns to reporting long speeches full of moral platitudes and "uplift"; a Cabinet Minister, however commonplace, was regarded as a lofty, almost unapproachable, being, and men like Macaulay and Gladstone were suffered, if not gladly, at least with respectful awe.

Albert was at once a firm believer in progress and an idealist. He dreamed of an England bathed in the pure light of reason—an England in which everyone acted from the highest motives. An orderly land, in which people took their pleasures in a fitting manner, neither drank, gambled nor swore, retired early to bed and relied on his "Memoranda" to guide their politics and settle every detail of their daily life. And he was constantly shocked to find that man is a primitive violent being almost entirely swayed by such unreasonable impulses as his interests and affections. *"Il faut pour servir les hommes, rejeter toute raison, comme un baggage embarrassant, et s'élever sur les ailes de l'enthousiasme. Si l'on raisonne, on ne s'envolera jamais,"* said Anatole France. England was a country peculiarly unfitted for a man of his type: she has always been ruled by sentiment; her people are a strange fascinating mixture of coarseness and refinement—the Elizabethans would go from a cock-fight to listen to the madrigals of Orlando Gibbons—and behind these conflicting facets she burns with a genius and spirituality all her own.

There is no doubt that Albert was a thoroughly good conscientious man. The title "Albert the Good", bestowed upon him by some of his admirers, was deserved. Perhaps "Albert the *Too* Good" would have described him more accurately. He had so few of the human frailties common to poor humanity and—unlike Christ, to Whom a recent writer rather unwisely compared him—had little sympathy with them. Yet he was a religious man, though, like most Lutherans, he disliked dogma and could not understand why churchmen quarrelled over it. Hence his complete failure to see Wilberforce's point of view in the Hampden Case. He detested the Roman Catholic Church, denouncing bitterly its "hypocritical and shifty methods". "She is peace-loving (?) and meek (?) and does not seek for power (!)", he sneered. He was desperately lonely. There is no loneliness so bitter as that of he who is conscious that even those who are nearest and dearest to him do not understand him. With the exception of Stockmar he had no friends outside his own family: and Stockmar was his evil genius. Of the two obstacles to his happiness the first and greatest was Stockmar, the other being the want of vitality caused by his weak stomach. He could have taken his stomach in hand and with care have made it behave reasonably, but Stockmar gave him no chance. He took *him* in hand instead and, with his infernal ambitions, his relentless slave-driving and his incessant admonition to "never relax", made him what he was; froze in him all the pleasant instincts of youth when he was yet but a boy and turned him not only into an efficient and wholly unnecessary— machine but, incidentally, into one of the most worried and unhappy of living men.

. . . . .

Stockmar had journeyed far. The uncouth son of the respectable Coburg lawyer, the obscure medical student, had become the adviser and confidant of kings; a man to whom the secret tortuous tracks of European diplomacy were open roads and whose advice turned the scales in many a momentous question of politics. He was the trusted friend of Leopold of Belgium and the power behind the throne in England. But happiness had eluded him, as, through him, it had eluded Albert. He was detested in England and Belgium and feared and distrusted in Germany. In 1858, when paying a visit to the Crown Prince and Princess, a friend of his with whom he had been seen crossing the bridge that leads from the palace at Potsdam was afterwards asked by Count K——: "Who was the man walking with you this morning?" "Stockmar," was the reply. "Ah!" said the Count, "then why on earth didn't you pitch him into the river?" In every country in which he carried on his underground activities he was believed to be spying on behalf of some other country. In Germany they said he had secret lodgings which were the headquarters of his spy system. He had, of course, many admirers. One of them wrote to him with true German simplicity: "Highly esteemed, thoughtful, deeply versed in all worldly wisdom, and nevertheless nobly simple friend!"

Needless to say, he was courted with the utmost servility. Though he avoided publicity as much as possible, his power was well known in Court and diplomatic circles, so he was inundated with requests to speak a word in high quarters for this or that person. Noblemen wrote begging his interest for themselves or their sons, and financiers tried anxiously to find out from him which way the political cat was likely to jump. He was not, however, very *serviable*. He might easily have accumulated a vast fortune, but, as we have seen, money was not his object—a fact singularly irritating to those for whom its acquisition is the be all and end all of life. There, they said, was this important and comparatively poor person, who could by lifting his finger have enriched both himself and them, and he refused to dance to their piping! So they hated him more than ever.

Stockmar, like Albert, was a good man. He had the quite human love of pulling strings, but he did not pull them to gratify his own personal ambitions. He was possessed with one all-consuming longing; to see a Germany united under Prussia and playing a leading part in the world. To that end he sacrificed himself (and Albert) and renounced all the sweet intimacies of family life, the laughter of children, the pleasant social round. And all in vain; for though he glimpsed the promised land he never reached it. Had he lived a few years longer, he would have seen his dreams come true; a proud united Germany under the rule of the arrogant Hohenzollerns—fully conscious of its own vast superiority over any other civilization this old world has ever seen. And again—if his anxious brooding spirit haunts the scenes where in life he schemed and laboured—he has witnessed in less than the short span of fifty years the utter collapse of the house of cards he had helped to build. *Vanitas, vanitatem!*

CHAPTER EIGHT

". . . many a time
I have been half in love with easeful death."
                                    KEATS.

"I do not cling to life."
                                    PRINCE ALBERT.

IN 1861 Albert and Victoria had been husband and wife
for twenty-one years. They did not underestimate their
value to humanity in general. Victoria wrote to Uncle
Leopold : "On Sunday we celebrated with feelings of deep
gratitude and love the twenty-first anniversary of our blessed
marriage, a day which has brought to us and, I may say,
to the world at large such incalculable blessings. Very few
can say with me that their husband at the end of twenty-one
years is not only full of the friendship, kindness and affection
that a truly happy marriage brings with it, but of the same
tender love as in the first days of our marriage." Alas,
very few indeed! But the clouds were gathering. Albert's
strength was obviously failing. The unremitting work he
inflicted on himself was sapping all the little vitality left in
a constitution never, as Stockmar had seen in early days,
very robust. He had many anxieties. Germany was not
behaving itself, but he hoped great things from the new
King of Prussia. "With a Prince prepared to take the lead,"
he wrote, "the German people will suffice for itself; nay,

it will even become a power which its neighbours, *The Times* included, will regard with respect."

There were family worries, too. The Duchess of Kent died. With the passing of the years the old lady had become reconciled to being a nonentity. Victoria had gradually made her understand that her influence was to count for nothing in political and Court life, and with that under-standing, which had been hard to acquire, had come about a renewal of the natural affection between mother and daughter. To mourn was almost a *métier* with Victoria, so she abandoned herself wholeheartedly to grief, leaving Albert to puzzle out the rather complicated affairs of the Duchess, arrange the funeral and answer the innumerable letters of condolence from friends, family and foreign royalties. "Victoria," he wrote to Stockmar, "is terribly nervous, and the children are a disturbance to her. By business I am wellnigh overwhelmed, as I do my best to save Victoria all trouble, while at the same time I am Mamma's sole executor." To add to these worries *The Times* attacked him on the Italian question, hinting that the liberation of Italy was being hindered by the Austrian predilections of the Court. Then, too, "Bertie" was a worry. He had been sent to Cambridge the previous year, and Cambridge found the task of educating him at least as difficult as his former tutors had done!

Albert was suffering badly from insomnia aggravated by toothache—dentists were less skilful in 1861 than they are nowadays. On November 22nd he went to inspect the new Military College at Sandhurst, in which he was greatly interested. It was a miserable day, cold and soaking wet, and he came back chilled to the bone and dead tired. The next day, though racked with rheumatic pains, he went out shooting—the day's programme must be adhered to: he had "never relaxed", and he never would while he could still crawl about. The following day he would have liked to rest, but news arrived from Cambridge that "Bertie", who did not suffer from his father's inability to relax, had been relaxing with highly undesirable companions! So to Cambridge he went post-haste to remonstrate with the frivolous youth and point a moral. There was a distressing scene. For once Albert lost his self-control, and he returned much upset. It was not surprising; he himself had never in his life indulged in youthful frivolities, and he was feeling thoroughly ill. He could neither eat nor sleep, and his favourite doctor, Dr. Baily, who knew his constitution, had been killed in a railway accident a few months before. So he was left to the mercies of that incompetent old muddler, Sir James Clark, who had so singularly failed to diagnose the illness of Lady Flora Hastings, and who was equally unsuccessful in his case. Victoria, curiously enough, had retained unbounded faith in Sir James's powers and had insisted on Albert's appointing him his chief physician. Though hardly able to drag one foot before another, Albert refused to give in and on the 29th November reviewed the Eton College Volunteers. It was madness on his part, and he knew it: he was playing with death, and death held all the cards. But he did not cling to a life which, though it had brought him power, honour, wealth, nearly everything, indeed, that men hold dear, had yet withheld happiness.

There was trouble with America—then in the throes of Civil War. The English steamer *Trent*, which had on board two envoys of the Southern States, was stopped by the captain of a northern man-of-war who insisted on the envoys being given up. Lord John Russell wrote a dispatch couched in such language that, had it been presented, it must have resulted in the breaking-off of diplomatic relations between the two countries. Albert saw this and, by altering it a little and introducing a spirit of conciliation, safeguarded the national honour while giving no cause of offence to the Americans. When he had finished his task he said to Victoria: "I am so weak I could hardly hold the pen." He had written his last Memorandum.

At long last he took to his bed, and Dr. Watson was called in. He at once diagnosed the mysterious illness as typhoid fever, dating from the drive to Sandhurst. From the first the case was hopeless. Even had he received proper treatment at the onset of the disease, it is doubtful if his enfeebled constitution could have withstood it. After a few days he asked to be taken to another room and, on reaching it, said: "Why, this is the room George IV and William IV died in"; and he did not forget that the only night on which Victoria had ever slept in it was the night the Duchess of Kent died. The fever did not run very high, and he was able to converse with Victoria. He stroked her hand, calling her *Gutes Weibchen* and other endearing names in German. She did not for a moment believe that she was going to lose him : only two days before his death she wrote reassuringly to Uncle Leopold. Had not the great Sir James told her that "everything was quite satisfactory"? Towards the evening of December 14th, however, his breathing became quick and laboured; his colour changed to a dusky grey and he arranged his hair with those weak gestures so often seen when the end is near—perhaps a subconscious effort to receive the Dread Visitor fittingly. Victoria, who had left the room for a short rest, was summoned in haste : but the long day of this troublous life was over for him; his work done. The dying lamp flickered for a moment . . . and expired.

When Victoria realized the truth, she uttered a despairing cry which rang through the hushed rooms of the Palace. That lamp had been the light of her life; only darkness remained. Love, happiness, ambition—all she held dear— had been centred in that quiet figure now lying folded in the awful peace of death.

"The chariot of Israel and the Horsemen thereof."

.　　.　　.　　.　　.

Messieurs, le temps me presse
Adieu, la compagnie.
Grâce à vos politesses!
"Le Juif Errant," old French Ballad.
ANON.

And Stockmar? Yes. *Grâce à vos politesses!* He did not want them; he never had wanted them. He did not deal in *politesses*! The death of the Prince Consort was a terrible blow to him. Albert had been his creation, his tool;

and now he was dead, ere the work for which he had destined him was accomplished. Had the Baron no misgivings? He had seen his pupil change from a simple ingenuous boy to a tired sick worried man, old at forty; and *he* had caused the change. He fell into a state of hypochondria, seeing only his sisters and a few old friends. To pass the long hours he sorted his papers and could hardly imagine that he had ever been in relation with many of even his most distinguished and prolific correspondents: he had forgotten their very handwriting. The complicated questions of which the letters treated had solved themselves, or remained unsolved; the play was over, and most of the actors dead.

"I must confess I was not prepared for such a miserable old age," he wrote. His stomach ached on for two years after the death of Albert, until, in 1863, a stroke of apoplexy removed him to a higher sphere, where, if there are pens in Heaven, he must surely be engaged in writing Memoranda on the politics of the celestial realms. When he had ceased to breathe his worthy *Frau*—who, poor soul, had been left so much to her own devices—carefully removed the elaborate nightgown in which he had been attired to receive the farewell visits of his friends: whether because having brought nothing into this world he should carry nothing out, or because in those days the garments in which one died were the perquisite of the undertaker— history does not relate. On his tombstone are the appropriate words:

"There is a friend that sticketh closer than a brother."

BISHOP SAMUEL WILBERFORCE

THE BEST OF BOTH WORLDS

(BISHOP SAMUEL WILBERFORCE)

CHAPTER ONE

"I am made all things to all men."
S. PAUL.

TO be known to the world and his wife by a nickname
generally indicates the possession of some marked
characteristic—pleasing or otherwise. Schoolboys have an
uncanny knack of hitting on names which exactly fit their
youthful owners and which they sometimes retain throughout their lives. Nicknames are, of course, common in any
close, intimate society and were particularly so in the
beginning of the nineteenth century when, apart from the
Services and the Church, politics offered the only career
open to a gentleman. The delightful Mr. Creevey has left
on record many of those bestowed on various politicians
and members of the highly important and aristocratic circle
in which—on an income of next to nothing a year—he
lived and moved and had his being. Though it is quite
likely that Lord Brougham, Western, Bexley and Sir Robert
Peel did not enjoy being called respectively "Beelzebub" or
the "Arch-Fiend", "Old Stiff Rump", "Mouldy", and
"Spinning Jenny", their reputations can hardly have
suffered through it. But to have earned—deservedly or
undeservedly—the nickname of "Soapy Sam" was distinctly
unfortunate for that amiable and distinguished prelate,

Bishop Samuel Wilberforce—no matter with how good a grace he answered to it. It may be, perhaps, not without interest to glance at the very active part he played in the ecclesiastical and social life of his day.

Samuel Wilberforce was born in 1805 at Clapham, then a dignified suburb and the centre of the Evangelical "Clapham Sect". His father was William Wilberforce, the "Emancipator of the Negro". Mr. Creevey writes of him in 1812: "I gave my vote to Wilberforce on account of his good conduct in Africa; a place returning no members to Parliament but still—from the extraordinary resemblance its inhabitants bear to human creatures—of some consequence." Wilberforce was one of those extremely pious and, at the same time, extremely practical evangelical public characters of whom we find so many in the first half of the nineteenth century. He gave his son much good advice, writing him long letters full of a curious mixture of piety and worldly wisdom. In one of them he advises the boy never to neglect to get acquainted with anyone who might be useful to him—advice which Samuel, to do him justice, never failed to follow. In another he recommends him to practise hospitality, saying that the giving of dinner- and supper-parties had made him very popular and more than repaid their expense in one way and another.

Samuel was a nice boy; affectionate, good at sports, and intensely amiable. Even as a child he could always see everyone else's point of view with regard to any question, trying to solve the little problems of daily life in a way that united Christian precepts and practical politics.

Unfortunately his father refused to send his sons to public schools, fearing that their morals might be contaminated. It was a pity. Eton would have done Samuel a world of good. He was educated privately and regretted it for the rest of his life. But the estimable man did not content himself with giving the boy good advice: he took enormous pains in training his memory and—being an old Parliamentary hand—taught him the art of speaking in public without notes and how to vary his language and make his subject interesting.

When Samuel was eighteen he went to Oxford—Oriel —of which college John Henry Newman and Edward Pusey were Fellows, and where, within two years, two youths who were to make their mark in the world, Henry Edward Manning and William Ewart Gladstone, became his fellow students. Naturally he soon distinguished himself in the "United Debating Society", now known as the "Union". His politics at that time were Liberal, but on taking Orders he decided to adopt the Conservative opinions then almost universal among the clergy. Later on, with that admirable toleration and spirit of compromise so desirable in a Dignitary of the Church, he became a Liberal-Conservative. On the second occasion on which he spoke, the subject of the debate was the deposition of Charles I. Samuel for once was on the side of the minority: he defended it. But, even so, he was living up to his convictions. Poor Charles was in a decided minority when they chopped off his head !

At Oxford Samuel's career was all that could be desired. He made excellent friends, carefully avoiding extremists of any set, whether in work, play or religion, and, though not by any means a great student, he took a first-class in mathematics and a second in classics. In 1828 he married Emily Sargent of Lavington, one of whose sisters married Henry Edward Manning—afterwards Cardinal Manning. The marriage was a very happy one and, as might be expected with the lucky Samuel, turned out well from a worldly point of view; for, although his bride had at that time two brothers living, they were both of them obliging enough to depart this life and by so doing gave their sister Emily possession of the family property. The honeymoon was spent in Switzerland, which they loved. All clergymen love Switzerland. It inspires them with charming metaphors for subsequent use in the pulpit; "awful majesty, ineffable purity, whiter than snow" and the like. They went to Mürren and gazed at the Jungfrau. "Such a sight of glory as made my blessed wife in 1828 seize my hand and say, 'Can that be earth?'" writes Wilberforce in his diary.

In the same year he was ordained, and in less than two years, when only twenty-five, he was appointed Rector of Brighstone in the Isle of Wight. "Why, they've sent us a boy!" said one of his parishioners, but after hearing his first sermon he changed his opinion. Another of his flock said that it was *impossible* to offend him. "He was a pleasant man in every way, in church and out of church."

Those were difficult times in England. Poverty and discontent were rife, and there was much anti-clerical feeling. Farmers everywhere were refusing to pay tithes,

and riots, in some cases—especially in the southern and
western counties—amounting almost to a reign of terror,
were common. In 1831, on November 5th, the effigies of
the Bishops of Exeter and Winchester were substituted for
Guy Fawkes and burnt outside their own palace gates. The
Bishop of Bristol fared worse: his palace was looted and
burnt to the ground.

That popular feeling should have been strong against the
Church was not surprising: it had long lost all its apostolic
zeal, and religion had become a respectable convention.
It was *"the thing"* to go to church at least once every Sunday
—the women showing off their smartest frocks and the men
their black coats and top hats: even the poorest classes had
their Sunday clothes.   Church and State walked hand in
hand, and livings that happened to be well endowed were
the prescriptive right of younger sons and family fools.
Those *not* so well endowed were reserved for deserving
young men who were, unfortunately, merely pious.   A
glance at the list of churchwardens during the eighteenth
and nineteenth centuries inscribed on the arches of St.
George's, Hanover Square, shows us with what approval
the Almighty was regarded by the "best people".   The
administration of the immense wealth of the Church was a
national scandal.   Rich bishops living in their palaces and
hand-in-glove with the county families; rich livings held,
as we have seen, by members of those same families, and
the well-paid and delightfully housed Deans and Canons
of cathedrals, contrasted painfully with livings of which
the miserable stipends meant semi-starvation for their

unfortunate holders and curates who could hardly keep body
and soul together. Trollope in "Framley Parsonage" gives
us an interesting picture of clerical life. We see the Rev.
Mark Roberts with his £900 a year living and his charming
Vicarage—he paid his curate £70 a year—and the Rev.
Charles Crawley in a neighbouring parish with his £130 a
year and house that was little more than a cottage. Vicars
of Wakefield were to be found all over England. The
snobbishness, too, of the Church of England was incredible.
Prince Albert, speaking to Lord Wriothesley Russell, Canon
of Windsor, expressed great anxiety that his chaplains
should be "gentlemanlike, fit for the palace"; and Lady
Lyttelton, writing to a friend in 1844, says: "Henry, is it
wrong or unusual for a gentleman to take a *paid* curacy?
George says Yes; Billy, No."

There was a good deal of dissent among the manu-
facturing and the poorer classes, but in the country and in
the county towns it did not pay to be a dissenter. Dissenting
tradesmen were not dealt with by the "Quality", and
dissenters were not employed by them. The wives of even
rich dissenters were not called on. Still they dared to be
Daniels, even in cathedral towns where many small tradesmen—chiefly greengrocers and cobblers—seemed to prefer
to "sit under" half-educated ministers in squalid little
buildings with corrugated iron roofs than to seek salvation
in the more gracious atmosphere of their cathedral. There
is a curious connection between greengrocery, shoe-repairing
and dissent. It would be interesting to trace it to its source.

Let us return to our Samuel, who did not allow himself

to be unduly disturbed by the unruly wills of sinful men. He stayed quietly in his vicarage and wrote a short "Tract on Tithes"—"to try and correct the prejudices of the lower order of farmers", as his son tells us. He also compiled a hymn-book for the use of his parish and, in collaboration with his brother Robert, wrote a life of his father. In sending a copy to Gladstone, he said: "There is no height to which you may not fairly rise in this country. . . . I would have you view yourself as one who may become the head of all the better feelings of the country. . . . I think my father's life beautifully shows that a deep and increasing personal religion must be the root of that deep and unwearied consistency in right which I have ventured to press on you."

Rather a didactic letter, perhaps, for one young man to write to another, but Samuel was quite sincere. He had entered the Church from conviction: it was his natural *métier*, and the fact that the family wealth and influence insured rapid preferment had played no part in his choice of a profession. He was, indeed, singularly fitted for it. A born preacher, good-looking, tactful, fond of sport and social life, he would have made his way even without the extraneous advantages he possessed. Then, too, he was never troubled with the theological doubts and intellectual hair-splittings of the super-sensitive and super-superstitious Newman. Nor did he, like Manning, wage perpetual war with ambition and with his conscientious scruples—a war in which conscience generally retired, if not beaten, at least half-persuaded that ambition would, if given its head, best

serve the inscrutable purposes of an all-wise providence!
Samuel throughout his life remained on the best of terms
both with the Church of England and with the Deity. The
Christian religion had as few difficulties for him as it had
for the hero of *Erewhon*, who wrote of his native servant
Showbok: "I used to catechise him by the camp-fire and
explain to him the mysteries of the Trinity and of original
sin, with which I was myself familiar, having been the
grandson of an Archdeacon by my mother's side, to say
nothing of the fact that my father was a clergyman of the
English Church." How crystal clear must those mysteries
have appeared to Samuel, *himself* an Archdeacon!

He loved Brighstone and Brighstone loved him. No
wonder; he was rich, eloquent and "so pleasant". But the
powers that be had not forgotten this eligible young parson.
Offers of preferment were showered upon him—among
others, St. Dunstan's in the West, Tunbridge Wells Chapel
and Leeds. In 1839 he was made Archdeacon of Surrey.
The following year he spoke at an anti-slavery meeting at
Exeter Hall and attracted the attention of Prince Albert,
who at the same meeting made the first of his interminable
series of dreary orations. "Who is he?" asked Albert and
within six months appointed him one of his chaplains. This
was only a beginning. The following year he was given a
canonry at Winchester Cathedral, and two months later
he accepted the important living of Alverstoke. Perhaps
Leeds, with its wide sphere of influence and its poverty-
stricken population, would have been the choice of a more
apostolic priest; but then, what an uncomfortable place, and

what a suffocating atmosphere! It was not to be thought
of. "How would your lamp burn?" wrote his friend
Bishop Sumner. "*Not an hour.* And just before, or just
after, your own would expire that of Emily, choked with
coal smoke." Alas! Breath has a regrettable habit of
failing us under even the most agreeable conditions. It failed
poor Emily, and in the unexceptionable air of Winchester,
shortly after Samuel had taken up his residence in the Close.

Albert liked his new chaplain; so, it goes without saying,
did Victoria, and so also did the Court. How well he
understood them all! Lady Lyttelton says in 1842: "I
never saw a more agreeable man, and if such a Hindu were
to be found, I think he would go near to convert me and
lead me to Juggernaut. He never parades his serious
feelings." And on other occasions: "The real delight of
this visit is the presence of Archdeacon Wilberforce."
"Archdeacon Wilberforce is gone, after preaching to us
yesterday at morning service a *most beautiful* sermon. It
was in manner and language the highest in eloquence, and
his voice and earnest simplicity all the time leave one no
wish except that one could remember every word and *oh!*
practise every precept. I was *so* pleased, sitting close behind
Prince Albert, to observe him nodding his head in warm
approbation repeatedly, and then turning round gently to
see if the Queen was equally impressed. Everybody says
he will be a Bishop, and so he ought."

There was some talk of his being appointed tutor to
the Prince of Wales—a post he would certainly not have
cared for. Says Lady Lyttelton: "The report—it is nothing

more yet, alas! and may be a dream—of his going to be tutor to Princey gains ground. . . . Said I to the Queen this morning: 'Madam! Mr. Wilberforce has asked leave to see the Prince of Wales—may he?' 'Oh, yes, by all means'; and then, after a little pause: 'I think he looked rather ill last night.' " Lady Lyttelton, thinking of her pupil, replied: "Why, Ma'am, he certainly was rather fretful at bedtime!"

Samuel threw himself into all the amusements of the Court, even playing chess with Albert on Sunday. "Most clergymen would not do it nowadays," is Lady Lyttelton's comment, "all did it in my time, and in point of fact it is quite harmless; but—but—I want something to set against the constant compliance and increasing charm, which continue quite irresistible. It may be only the 'beauty of holiness'?" Lady Lyttelton seemed to have had her doubts, but they all fled directly he began to preach. He left her *"quite a rag. Such* a stream of Heavenly truth, *such* a flow of honeyed words"! But she laments that he is growing fat from too much dining out. On one occasion only she was disappointed in him. He had preached on the Crucifixion, and she thought the subject floored him. Her doubts with regard to the evening at chess would perhaps have been dissipated had she seen the entry in Samuel's diary recording the Sunday in question.

"Sunday, February 9. Finished sermon. 'God did tempt Abraham.' Preached it. Interview with Prince. Queen came in. Much talk—Peel's Church measures— Gladstone, sermons, why so dull? 'No object' Sir R. Peel, and Whitehall Chapel. After dinner long talk. Chess evening which I regret, not that my own conscience offended at it one jot, but that capable of misconstruction and not unlikely to receive it from Lady ——"

From Lady ——! Could it have been from Lady Lyttelton herself?

He had a pretty wit. "We were talking of hypnotism one evening after dinner," Lady Lyttelton says. "Fixing the eyes on some uninteresting object with undivided attention will cause it, I said." Samuel replied that he hardly thought so, as in that case the hypnotic sleep would occur frequently in church, as people were apt to look at the preacher. Both Victoria and Albert delighted in Samuel's conversation, and he took an equal delight in their society. He discussed astronomy with Victoria and was astonished, as well he might be, at her grasp of the subject. "Off to breakfast with Bunsen and then to Palace," he writes in his diary in 1841. "Prince *would* see me: showed me the young Duke of Cornwall[1] asleep in bassinet. Duchess of Kent 'wished to be introduced'. She very gracious, but speaks English poorly." He spent the week-end at Windsor after preaching and writes: "It was curious to see (for I contemplated myself objectively and free from the consciousness of subjectivity) sitting round the Queen's table the Queen, the Prince, Lord Melbourne, Archdeacon, Lady F. Howard, Baron Stockmar, Duchess of Kent, Lady Sandwich." He talked of literature with Stockmar—Coleridge and German authors—and found Stockmar "a

---

[1] Afterwards King Edward VII.

very superior man". Albert, too, he thought intelligent, right-minded and pleasing. "After breakfast, with the Prince for three-quarters of an hour; talk about Sunday. Told him I thought the 'Book of Sports' did more than almost anything to shock the English mind. He urged English want of amusements for common people of an innocent class—no *gardens*. 'In Coburg'—ah, yes, it was very different—'thirty-two gardens frequented by different sorts of people who meet and associate in them.' 'I never have heard a real shout in England. All my German servants marry because they say it is so dull here; nothing to interest—good living, good wine, but there is nothing to do but turn rogue or marry.' "

Samuel was finding life decidedly agreeable.

CHAPTER TWO

Tell wit how much it wrangles
in tickle points of nycenesse,
Tell wisedome she entangles
her-selfe in ouer wisenesse.

SIR WALTER RALEIGH.

PROMOTION, we are told, "cometh neither from the East nor from the West". . . . To many of us the North and the South are equally unpropitious. But to the Samuel Wilberforces of this world it is wafted on every breeze that blows. In 1845 Samuel was made Dean of Westminster, but he did not stay long at the Abbey, for a few months later, at the age of only forty, he accepted the Bishopric of Oxford. In the letter conveying the offer Peel said, "Her Majesty was graciously pleased, with many kind expressions towards yourself on her own part and on that of the Prince, fully and cordially" to sanction the choice. Albert honoured him with a personal letter of congratulation, and, as may be imagined, the Prince of Platitudes did not miss the chance of improving the occasion: "Let him (the Bishop) never forget the insufficiency of human knowledge and wisdom and the impossibility of any man (not an Albert!) or any Church to say, 'I am right, and I alone am right'. Let him, therefore, be meek and liberal, and tolerant to other confessions, but let him never forget that he is a representative of the Church of the land, the maintenance of which is as important to the country as that of its constitution or throne. Let him, therefore, always be conscious that the Church has duties to fulfil; that it does not exist for itself, but for the people, for the country, and that it ought to have no higher aim than to be the Church of the people. Let there be, therefore, no calling for new rights, privileges, grants, etc., but show the zeal and capacity of the Church to stretch her powers and capabilities to the utmost for the fulfilment of her sacred duties to the people in ministering and teaching."

Excellent advice though poorly expressed, but one wonders if it had not occurred to this young German, aged twenty-six, that the Dean of Westminster, aged forty, might possibly have himself formed some idea of his episcopal duties. That his essay was, to say the least of it, somewhat presumptuous did not, of course, enter his head; he must have a finger in every pie. He need not have worried: Samuel took his duties very seriously. His own conception of them reads very differently from that of the egregious Albert. Before his consecration he "marked down a few practical rules" for his own guidance. "The first great necessity seems to me to maintain a devotional temper. The first great peril—*secularity*. To guard against this by self-examination and, above all, by living in prayer. Remember that

> To serve God,
> In His way,
> Through His Grace,
>   is all.

"Now trusting in God's help, without which I well know by my own experience that all attempts at spending time devotionally are utterly vain, I resolve—

"First Resolution: As my universal rule when not hindered by illness or some impossibility, to secure at least one hour before breakfast for devotional exercises.

"Next, as my great fear is acting with *an eye to men and myself, rather than God*, I resolve—

"Second Resolution: Often to set my account, principles, etc., in the light of the coming day: and try thus to form the habit of acting under God's eye.

"Third Resolution: To form a regular systematic habit of intercessions for my clergy, etc. Be a 'father in God' to men of all opinions among my clergy. Take *time* to answer letters. Give no opinion on hearing one side. Beware of confiding—of speaking on feeling."

Another excellent memorandum—not in the Albertian sense!—was headed: Cautions—Never speak of clergy before servants or children. N.B.—*Never talk about them at all!* Never hurry men who come to consult you. Mere venting themselves is a relief.

From the first Samuel was a great success as a Bishop. He was a hard worker. Unlike Bishop Whately, who, plucking his lawn sleeves, said: "I don't know how it is, but when we have got these things on we never do anything else," he looked on his new appointment as the means of playing a leading *rôle* in Church matters. Bishop Whately, however, was the Bishop who is reported to have said that only once had he risen early, and that on that occasion he was so proud all the morning and so sleepy all the afternoon that he never repeated the experiment. Samuel may be said to have founded a new fashion in bishops—the busy, bustling energetic prelate of this twentieth century in which both spiritual and temporal Princes put in considerably more hours' work a day than does the average navvy.

He was always at the disposal of his clergy. At Cuddesdon—which he subsequently converted into a theological college for the training of candidates for ordination—he invited the Archdeacons and Rural Deans of his Diocese to stay with him in turn, two at a time, in order that he might go through the lists of their clergy and parishes and learn all the local conditions. Neither did he neglect the rich. Whenever he had to visit a parish where there was a great house, he took care to write informing the owner of his intentions. The letter was generally acknowledged by an invitation to dine and sleep. His genial manner made him extraordinarily popular, and his natural tact and charm were supplemented by keen powers of observation. On one occasion, when visiting the rector of a country village, he asked his host: "How is that jolly little white pony of yours?" The rector was highly gratified at the inquiry and took the Bishop to see it. "How on earth did you know he had a white pony?" said Sam's chaplain, who had accompanied him. "Oh, that was easy," was the reply, "his coat was covered with white horse-hairs." The candidates at Cuddesdon adored him. One of them once said to a group of friends: "If the Bishop said to me, 'I am going to the Cannibal Islands to-morrow: will you come?' I would go directly." "So would we," said they all in chorus.

His tact never failed him. Those were the days when Evangelical parsons wore Black Gowns and considered the surplice a Popish Vestment; indeed, they were quite convinced that Anti-Christ on his coming would be wearing one. Now, it happened that Samuel had promised to preach on the occasion of the reopening of a church that had just been restored. There was a procession of clergy, and all but two wore surplices. The two recalcitrants flatly refused to wear them, saying that nothing on earth would induce them to dally with the Scarlet Woman.

"What *can* I do?" said the rector to Samuel, who answered: "Leave it to me; they will wear surplices like the rest." Going up to one of them, he said: "Mr. ——, will you kindly read the First Lesson?" and to the other: "Will you read the Second Lesson?" Overwhelmed with delight, they fled to the Vestry to don the garment of perdition and from thenceforth ate out of their Bishop's hand.

Tact that amounted to courage was shown by him at a function in an industrial town where anti-clerical feeling ran high. On setting out for the church, he and the vicar with whom he was staying found the road leading to it thronged with an unmistakable crowd of roughs. Samuel took off his hat and, addressing them, said that the Superintendent of Police had offered him an escort but that he had declined, being sure that the townspeople would be ready to act as his body-guard if necessary—"I was not mistaken," said he, "and accordingly it is with confidence that I now commend myself and this my following to your guidance and respect." *Noblesse oblige.* They cheered him.

His capacity for being agreeable seemed to increase daily. "What do you *wish* me to say to them?" he would ask the rector of the church in which he was preaching, and he invariably said it. "How skilfully he adapts what he has to say to the circumstances of the locality and the people," cried his admirers. A Confirmation at Eton, a workhouse treat, a village church, or a girls' school; it was all the same to him, and yet —— a few people had misgivings. Was he, perhaps, *too* amiable, *too* anxious to please everybody, *too* fond of visiting the houses of the great? they asked and murmured something about the difficulty of serving God and Mammon.

Samuel came to Oxford at a difficult moment. The Oxford Movement was coming to a crisis, and this peace-loving man found himself between the devil of the Evangelical party and the deep sea of the Tractarians. The former accused him of having Romish tendencies, while Newman and his followers thoroughly distrusted him. There could hardly exist two individuals more utterly unlike each other than were the dreamy unworldly Newman and the new Bishop. As a matter of fact—and in this he was fully justified—Samuel took sides with neither party. "I am," he said, "for the party of the Church of England, and nothing narrower." He stood for the simplicity and dignity of the Cathedral service, so admirably suited to the indiosyncrasy of the English people, and of which Greville in 1834 wrote: "Went to St. Paul's yesterday to hear Sydney Smith preach. . . . The service is exceedingly grand, performed with all the pomp of a Cathedral and chanted with beautiful voices. The lamps scattered few and far between throughout the vast space under the dome, making darkness visible and dimly revealing the immensity of the building, were exceedingly striking. The Cathedral service thus chanted and performed is my *beau ideal* of religious worship— simple, intelligible, and grand, appealing at the same time to the reason and the imagination. I infinitely prefer it to the Catholic service, for though I am fond of bursts of music and clouds of incense, I can't endure the indistinguishable sounds which the priest mumbles over the prayers." Greville, by the way, was amazed by what he calls "the phenomenon" of the Roman Catholic Church, being at the same time "disgusted, hypnotized, forced into admiration, repelled and mystified." Its dishonesty and unscrupulousness shocked him, but he was always interested.

The story of the Oxford Movement has been told often enough, and never better than by Lytton Strachey in his masterly sketch of Cardinal Manning in *Eminent Victorians*. Started by the saintly Keble, who had inherited Catholic doctrine from his father, and who—while himself going to no extremes—handed them on to his pupils—among whom was the brilliant and erratic Hurrell Froude, brother of James Anthony Froude the historian. Froude, in his turn, discussed them with his friend Newman. The seed fell on good ground. Newman had been born four hundred years too late; his mind was wholly medieval. He longed passionately to see the Church the supreme authority in the land; to have Kings and nobles submitting humbly to its decrees; to see it producing Saints—even a few martyrs would not have come amiss to him—so he rushed into the fray with enthusiasm. The State had not created the Church; why should it claim the right to control it? His subtle analytical mind revelled in the mysteries of the Sacraments. He lived in an atmosphere cloudy with incense, through which floated visions of Sienese Madonnas. His mind was obsessed with the fascination of the Middle Ages, and his nights were spent studying the writings of the early fathers and the lives of the Saints.

In 1833 he began to publish the famous *Tracts for the Times*. They were a trumpet call to the Church to throw off her comfortable lethargy, to reject the authority of the State and to return to the practices of medieval Catholicism. There were tracts professing to distinguish between the Catholicism of the Anglican Church and the Roman branch, on "Reserve in communicating Religious Knowledge", on Fasting, and on Baptismal Regeneration. But the climax was reached in "Tract XC" in which he tried to prove that there was no essential difference between the true Catholic Church and the Anglican Church. To support his contention he seized on the Thirty-nine Articles, turned them inside out and with true Jesuitical casuistry twisted them into any shape that suited his purpose. Previous to this he had been joined by Dr. Pusey, a Canon of Christ Church, a brilliant scholar and a man of wealth, who was afterwards to become leader of the Movement. It is easy to understand how Newman with his burning fervour, his golden oratory and his medieval magic attracted the romantic youth of the thirties. Recruits flocked to his standard. Like the historic "Curate of Crief" they swallowed whole the most extreme dogmas, Saints, Miracles, Purgatory, Hell, Holy Oil and Holy Water filled them with ecstasy, and they confessed their sins with delicious tremors. But the effect on the country generally was very different. England was violently anti-Catholic, and Tract XC roused the Evangelical party to fury. Cries of "No Popery" rang through the land, and questions were asked in Parliament. Newman and his followers were accused, and with reason, of double-dealing, and, when in 1845—the year Wilberforce became Bishop of Oxford—he (Newman) finally collapsed into the Roman Catholic Church, he was attacked from all sides.

It is not surprising, when one considers the state of public feeling, that the Tractarians tempered their valour with discretion; but some of their methods can hardly be justified under any system of ethics. There is no doubt that Newman had fully accepted Roman Catholicism long before he was formally received into the Church of Rome. In the beginning he had abused it root and branch, writing among other things—"True, Rome is heretical now"—that she had "bound herself by a perpetual bond to Anti-Christ", that she was "cruel, lying, ambitious", "that we must flee from her as from a pestilence". And yet a few years later we find him writing to Pusey. "An idea has revived in my

mind of building a monastic house in this place", the place
being Littlemore where he subsequently bought some land,
built a house and gathered a few faithful followers around
him. But, when his Bishop wrote him a kind, dignified
letter asking if the reports as to his monastic intentions were
true, he replied indignantly denying the truth of the rumour.
The clerical mind, however, is fearfully and wonderfully
made. Newman, in his book on the Arians, quotes with
approval Clement of Alexandra, who said that "A Christian
both thinks and speaks the truth *except when careful treatment is necessary*, and then he will lie or, rather, *utter a lie,*
as the sophists say". Towards the end of his life he wrote his
famous *"Apologia Pro Vita Sua"*, in order to refute the
charges of dishonesty brought against him. It is one of the
most brilliant and, at the same time, most unconvincing
books ever written. He devotes a long chapter to the subtle
question "When is a lie not a lie?" a chapter he evidently
delighted in writing. In reading it, one can only feel that
the writer did "protest too much".

Manning was equally shifty, and character—hard,
self-centred and ambitious—was far less attractive than that
of Newman, to whom, indeed, he subsequently behaved
with an almost incredible cruelty and meanness. When
visiting Rome in 1848, he knelt when the Pope's carriage
was passing, though still an Archdeacon of the Church of
England. Two years before he went over to Rome, he wrote,
"Anglicanism as a theology, still more as the Church or the
faith, has so faded out of my mind that I cannot say I
reject it, but I know it no more. *I simply do not believe it.*

THE BEST OF BOTH WORLDS

I can form no basis, outline, or defence for it." But he
continued to take his wages as a minister of the Anglican
Church. Gladstone said of him in 1895: "I won't say
Manning is insincere. God forbid! But he is not
simple and straightforward." Then there is Faber, another
of their leaders, who kissed the feet of the Pope and said:
"The nearest approach I can make to Heaven is that it is
like Rome."

With all these extremists Samuel had but little sympathy.
He loved the *via media* in everything, and—what must have
seemed odd to Newman and his friends—he thought that,
having sworn at his ordination to be loyal to the Church,
he should keep faith with it. But, though he disliked the
Ritualistic excesses of Pusey's disciples, he fully appreciated
the spiritual vitality for which they stood. He felt that there
was room in the Anglican Church for all shades of opinion
honestly held. "The Church of England," he said, "is
not a Church of compromise but a Church of comprehension embracing within her fold men of every view between
those who absolutely deny her primary principles and those
who hold the doctrine of the Roman Catholic Church
which she has expressly condemned. In that comprehension
her strength lies."

It was not long before Samuel came into conflict with
Pusey, with whose views he differed radically. Pusey had
edited some Roman Catholic devotional books which Samuel
considered as unhealthy—if not actually perverting—and
as advocating the practice of Confession, of which he
thoroughly disapproved. "Private Confession and Absolu-

tion," he said, "are only fit for certain cases, they should never be enjoined as a necessary condition; they are very dangerous as a rule, as (1) tending to defile the soul by forcing it to dwell upon, put into words and speak to another what is far better rejected as a whole with loathing (2) tending in other cases to cause habitual prevarication and holding back, and also tending to place the priest instead of Christ instead of making his office lead on to Christ." Until these matters were settled he requested Pusey not to preach in the diocese of Oxford. The result was that most of the books to which he objected were withdrawn, and he revoked the inhibition: rather unwisely, perhaps, from the point of view of discipline, as he had no reason to suppose that the leopard had changed his spots. He wrote to Pusey in 1850: "You seem to me to be habitually assuming the place and doing the work of a Roman Confessor and not that of an English Clergyman. Now, I so firmly believe that of all the curses of Popery this is the crowning curse, that I cannot allow voluntarily within my charge the continuance of a ministry which is infected by it." He said that confession frequently encouraged immorality by making those who had hitherto been innocent of it familiar with the details and so poisoning their minds. Fasting Communion he also considered dangerous, saying that the *dicta* of St. Chrysostom on the subject were deliberately misconstrued.

He was equally emphatic with regard to the Sisterhoods, some of which—notoriously the one under Pusey's great friend Miss Seldon—were run on quite medieval lines, and which gave rise to a great deal of scandal. The "Mother Superior" (or "Lady Abbess", as Miss Seldon might well have been called) and the Father Confessor (Pusey himself) exacted from the Sisters treatment as humble and reverent as that given to Abbesses and Bishops in the Middle Ages. The Sisters were subjected to the most severe discipline. Some of them, who subsequently escaped from it, described it as "a Hell on Earth". Samuel wrote with regard to these institutions: "We cannot allow the Sisters to practise continual confession to, or to erect into directors, the wardens or chaplains of our House. . . . If Sisterhoods cannot be maintained except on a semi-Romanist scheme with its perpetual Confessions and its un-English tone, I am perfectly convinced that we had better have no Sister-hoods."

In 1850 the Pope, persuaded by Dr. Wiseman, the Roman Catholic Archbishop of Westminster ("that smooth oily priest" as Greville calls him) that England was ready to abjure its heresies and return to Mother Church, issued a Brief decreeing the re-establishment of a hierarchy of Bishops. This in itself was of small importance, but what *did* matter was the arrogance and impertinence of the language in which the Brief was couched. England was graciously informed that it had been "restored to its orbit in the ecclesiastical firmament from which its light had long vanished, and begun anew its course of regularly adjusted action round the centre of Unity, the source of jurisdiction, of light and of vigour"! Dr. Wiseman added fuel to the fire by writing a bombastic pastoral *"given from without*

143

the Flaminian Gate of Rome"! Those with a sense of humour smiled and wondered if Pio Nono was a wit or only a half-wit; but the Papal pretensions caused the British public, above all the Evangelical party, to see red. Albert, quick to seize the occasion, wrote a long memorandum. But, as a matter of fact, both he and Victoria disliked and feared Pusey and his followers far more than they disliked the Roman Catholics.

Greville wrote: "the Pope has been ill-advised on the Bishop question, and very impolitic. The whole proceeding on the part of the Papal Government has been mischievous and impertinent and deserves the severest censure. Wiseman, who ought to have known better, aggravated the question by his imprudent—not to say impudent—manifesto." Wiseman took fright later and drew up a loyal address to be signed by ecclesiastics and laymen, which he sent to Greville, requesting him to look it over. Greville told him it was all very well as far as it went but advised him to order the Bishops to sign their names only and omit all allusions to their Sees. Wiseman acted on this suggestion, and the storm blew over. Though a kindly enough old man, he had a curious faculty of irritating people. Lady Bloomfield writes indignantly of his remarks on the misery of the "purlieus of Westminster". "As for the poverty and dirt of Rome, it exceeds all belief," she says, "and, when Cardinal Wiseman talks of the purlieus of Westminster, I only wish he would turn his attention to those of the Vatican." He might, too, have suggested to Pio Nono that some of the more obviously faked relics should be removed. Lady Bloomfield saw at

St. John Lateron the table used at the last Supper, the Well of Samaria and a block of granite representing the height of our Lord.

It was unfortunate that Samuel's appointment to the See of Oxford should have coincided with the religious crisis through which that diocese was passing and also with the tendency towards Rome which followed the secession of Newman; for in many ways he was totally unfitted to cope with the situation. It needed a scholar deeply versed in ancient and modern divinity; and he was anything but that. It needed a strong man; one who, having resolved on a certain line of conduct, pursued it consistently to the end. And there again he failed. His very tolerance, amiability and spirit of compromise—qualities invaluable in themselves—were a stumbling-block to him. Torn between the narrow-minded suspicions of the unctuous Evangelicals and the excesses of the intractable Tractarians, he neither satisfied nor gained the respect of either party. He would out of sheer unwillingness to give offence, allow the one to use practices of which he disapproved—only to withdraw his permission in order to conciliate the other. And in the choice of his lieutenants he was too much swayed by his personal predilections. His own family, too, did not make things easier for him; two of his brothers went over to Rome.

Personally he was Anglican to the backbone. "There is a growing feeling," he wrote, "which I can only describe as an 'ashamedness' of the Anglican Church, as if our grand old Anglican Communion contrasted unfavourably with the Church of Rome. The habitual language held by many men sounds as if they were ashamed of our Church and its position; it is a sort of apology for the Church of England as compared with the Church of Rome. *Why, I would as soon think of apologizing for the virtue of my Mother to a Harlot!*"

As regards the work of the diocese he was wholly admirable. During his reign the See was greatly enlarged—Berkshire and Buckinghamshire being added to it. He found it in a very backward condition. Only seventeen livings—and these of small value—were in the gift of the Bishop. He left the number at one hundred and three, which included many of the most important town livings. He was responsible for the building and restoration of nearly four hundred Churches, and he put the Rite of Confirmation on an entirely new footing. He cared little for the deference and formality with which the average Bishop used to be surrounded. A senior member of the University said of him: "I remember when a Bishop of Oxford never drove into Oxford without four horses and two powdered footmen; and what does Sam do? He gets upon a horse and rides in by himself without so much as a groom behind him!"

Possibly his laxity with regard to ritualistic practices of which he did not approve was partly due to his conviction of the very real service that the Anglo-Catholic Movement, as it is now called, was rendering to the Church. Walter Besant in his "Fifty Years Ago" gives us an interesting picture of the average Church Service in the thirties. The musical part of it was, he tells us, "taken slow—incredibly slow; no one now who is not old enough to remember would believe how slow it was. The voluntary at the beginning was a slow rumble; the Psalms were very slowly read by the clergyman and the Clerk alternately, the *Gloria* alone being sung; also to a slow rumble. The Choir was generally stationed in the organ loft, (*Anglo-Catholics, copying Rome, are trying to revive the objectionable custom*) which has been known to be built over the altar at the East End— as at Great St. Mary's, Cambridge—but was generally at the West End. It was not a choir of boys and men only, but of women and men. The *'Te Deum'* was always 'Jackson' —from my youth up I have loathed 'Jackson'; there was just one lively bit in it for which we looked and waited, but it lasted a very few bars, and then the thing dragged on more slowly than ever till it came to the welcome words, 'Let me never be confounded'. Two hymns were sung— very slowly; they were always of the kind which expressed either the despair of the sinner or the doubtful joy of the believer. I say doubtful, because he was constantly being warned not to be too confident; not to mistake a vague hope for the assurance of election, and because he was always being told how few in number were the elect, and how extremely unlikely that there could be many of these few in that one flock." There were many kind of preachers, he tells us. The dry, the eloquent, the low, the threatening, the scholarly; but they all preached Hell and damnation; the cruel Father, and the Son who could help but a few. They loved to depict the despairing deathbeds of the careless and the agony of the bereaved for one "cut off in his sins". Hell seems to have been the spiritual home of many of these clerical gentlemen; one Evangelical divine of the mid-nineteenth century, who had evidently been favoured with inside information, informed his congregation that it was paved with unbaptised babies!

The clergy of those days took their duties very easily, visiting little except among their rich parishioners and—in the country—hunting and shooting. There was one evening service a week, and the various guilds, societies and church organizations of to-day were unknown. Even the most important Saints' Days were neglected. But the parson was generally a scholar and a gentleman and sincere enough according to his lights.

The Tractarians were tremendously in earnest, and it is not too much to say that they gave the Church a new life and a deep spirituality which it had long lacked and to which, in many ways, it is nowadays a stranger. The effect, too, that the Oxford Movement had in brightening Services, bringing warmth, sympathy and colour into them, and in improving the music, is incalculable. Then, too, it has brought interest into the lives of thousands of emotional youths of the less fortunate classes, who love dressing up, carrying banners and swinging censers. As for the elderly maiden ladies for whom it has provided an engrossing occupation, their name is legion!

In these days of little faith it is difficult for us to understand the passionate feelings aroused by religious questions a hundred years ago. Lady Lyttelton writes in 1850:

"How ashamed one feels that the difference of a candle, or a bow, or a black or white dress, should influence our soul's belief and feelings!"

During all these excitements Samuel became more and more popular in the great world. He was, with the exception perhaps of Liddon, the most popular preacher in England. He was equally popular as a diner out. He had an endless store of anecdotes, and his wit and social charm made him the darling of society. At Court, too, he was *personna gratissima*. "The Bishop is very agreeable and brilliant as usual," says his enthusiastic admirer, Lady Lyttelton, "and, I fancy, a little graver, which I am glad of."

But the Royal Sun was soon to cease shedding its rays on Samuel. In the autumn of 1847 came the Hampden affair, which caused almost as much excitement in the clerical dovecotes as did the Oxford Movement.

CHAPTER THREE

O N November 15th 1847 orthodox Churchmen were
shocked to the soul on reading in *The Times* that
Lord John Russell had recommended Her Majesty to
appoint Dr. Hampden to the vacant See of Hereford.

Hampden in 1832 had, by his "Bampton Lectures" (in
which he was considered to have enunciated doctrines of a
Socinian tendency), set Oxford by the ears. He had aggravated his offence with a pamphlet published two years later
entitled "Some observations on Religious Dissent". For
this the Convocation of the University censured him by
474 votes against 94. Notwithstanding his unpopularity,
Lord Melbourne, with the peculiar sardonic humour so
entirely his own, appointed him in 1836 Regius Professor
of Divinity, and, when Lord John capped it all by making
him a bishop, the clerical kettle boiled over with indignation.
Both clergy and laity all over the country were thrown into
a ferment. Meetings were held; petitions poured in; it was
an insult to the Church, the University, the public. *The
Times* wrote: "We cannot imagine on what principle or
motive it has been adventured". Thirteen Bishops, including our Samuel, signed a protest to Lord John Russell—who
had also been attacked by the Archbishop of Canterbury—
though none of them brought any specific charges against
Hampden.

Samuel wrote to Mr. Anson (Albert's Secretary): "You have no doubt read *The Times* article on Dr. Hampden. I am afraid it is only too true. I cannot conceive *what* was Dr. Hampden's recommendation. He was not a persecuted man, for he had got a station far higher than he ever dreamed of already; he is not an able or an active man, or one popular with any party, and unless Lord John Russell wished for an opportunity of shocking the young confidence of the Church in him, I cannot conceive why he should have made it. I deeply lament it. S. Oxon."

It was not the first time that Lord John had been unfortunate in his choice of bishops, and it furnished occasion for the epigram:

> Lord John had bishops to provide,
> And chose—two precious Turks.
> One bishop for his *Faith* was tried;
> The other, for his *Works*.[1]

For no one, however, was the appointment more unfortunate than it was for Samuel. He wrote a long letter to Lord John, begging him to reconsider his decision; but to no effect. The rectory of Ewelme (which Hampden held as Regius Professor) being in his diocese, he was forced to take a leading part in the controversy, and he was temperamentally unfitted to cope with the responsibility. The devil himself could not have contrived a situation more fraught with danger for him, and in the end he succeeded in seriously injuring not only his own reputation but also his cause.

---

[1] The Bishop of Manchester.

His first step was to beg Lord John to give Hampden the chance of refuting the charges brought against him, but Lord John considered that this was none of his business. The University had in the meantime formulated its grievances and applied to Samuel to sign "Letters of Request", in order that the case might be brought before the Court of Arches. Samuel refused, saying that he had no wish to "promote any suit against Dr. Hampden" but that if such a case were started in the Consistory Court of the diocese of Oxford he would sign the "letters". Dr. Hampden took the matter with a high hand and wrote a letter to Lord John complaining of Tractarian persecution and asserting his entire orthodoxy; on which Samuel signed the "Letters of Request" and gave his sanction to the case being submitted to the Court of Arches, where definite charges would be made which Hampden would be obliged to answer.

Had Samuel now left things to take their course, all would have been well; but, alas for him! his fatal spirit of compromise urged him to try and undo what he had done. He wrote to the promoters of the suit begging *them* to withdraw the "Letters" on condition that he obtained from Hampden satisfactory explanations of some of the offending passages in the "Bampton Lectures" and the "Observations on Religious Dissent". And he wrote a letter to Hampden formulating certain theological points to which he required Hampden's consent, at the same time begging *him* to withdraw the offensive publication.

He obtained no satisfaction. Hampden's blood was now

up, and he had put himself into the hands of a lawyer. As regards the "Observations", too, he was on solid ground. They were being sold against his wish. Samuel lost his head and made blunder after blunder. He first tried to negotiate with the contemptuous Hampden, through the Provost of Oriel, and, on being again snubbed, ate his own words. He then wrote to Hampden saying that he had carefully studied the "Bampton Lectures" in the light of certain explanations that the author had deigned to furnish since their original publication and admitting that he had come to the conclusion that they did not justly warrant the suspicions of unsoundness to which they had given rise; that in fact they were as innocuous as milk and honey; food, indeed, for religious babes! The inevitable result was, of course, that both sides turned on him and accused him of hypocrisy, vacillation and incompetence. And all the time he was only being his tolerant, rash, impetuous, generous, unjudicial self. Greville, who did not like him, wrote: "the Hampden affair has been greatly to the advantage of the doctor; his enemies have exposed themselves in the most flagrant manner, and Archdeacon Hare has written a very able pamphlet exposing the rascality—for that is the proper word—of his accusers, and affording his own valuable testimony to Hampden's orthodoxy. Above all things Sly Sam of Oxford—my would-be director and confessor—has covered himself with ridicule and disgrace. His disgrace is the greater because everybody sees through his motives; he has got into a scrape at Court and is trying to scramble out of it. However, he is found out, and his favour seems to have long been waning." He goes on to say that the Queen and Albert are in a state of hot zeal. "Albert writes to Lord John Russell every day to try and persuade him to take action"—which of course Lord John did not do. Most of the clergy who joined in the outcry, he tells us, had never read a word of Hampden's writings: "Now they are set forth, and people see his unintelligible jargon about dogmas themselves unintelligible. There must be fair-minded people who are disgusted with the whole affair and at the ferocity with which these holy disputants assault and vituperate each other about that which none of them understand and which is a mere mockery and delusion to say that any of them believe it. It is cant, hypocrisy, and fanaticism from beginning to end. There is that fawning old sinner, the Bishop of Exeter, who actually called on Hampden at Oxford to congratulate him on the very lectures—the Bampton—which he was now condemning."

That many of the "holy disputants" held widely different opinions as to the theological dogmas in dispute is more than likely, most of the latter being, like the Trinity, incomprehensible; but at all events they enjoyed the row. It was, they felt, a family affair, and they conducted it with all the acrimony customary in quarrels among relations. But that Albert should have put in his spoke was inexplicable to those who did not know their Albert. His narrow Lutheran mind was quite incapable of understanding these metaphysical subtleties, and his intense German Protestantism caused him to condemn, *a priori*, dogma of any description. It seemed to him ridiculous that Samuel

should have objected to Hampden's appointment on such
trivial grounds. When Samuel withdrew his opposition,
he was fully convinced that he only did so in order to
remain in favour at Court and professed to believe that
worldly considerations alone kept him from going over to
Rome. Lord Aberdeen tried to reason with him and was
met with the remark: "He has a motive for all he does."
"Yes, Sir," said Lord Aberdeen, "but what a bad motive?"
There was still intercourse—Windsor being in the Diocese
of Oxford and Samuel holding the post of Almoner to the
Order of the Garter—but the old intimacy was over, and
poor Samuel was treated with marked coldness by Victoria
and her lord and master.

What, one wonders, did Lady Lyttelton think of it all?
Perhaps it is not difficult to guess. She had one of those
minds so common at Court; minds that take their colour
wholly from their surroundings. She was honestly convinced that all light, learning and piety flowed from the
Royal Luminaries in whose rays she basked and that those
on whom the said Luminaries ceased to shine were worthy
of nothing but to be cast into outer darkness. At any rate,
after the Hampden affair she refers only once to Samuel,
and in rather a catty manner: "I shall make known to the
Queen that Mrs. Conyngham Ellis's book has arrived, when
it shall have arrived, and also explain what it is. And
assuredly I do not think her 'impertinent' for sending it *to
me*. I do think her rather *officious*, as I do all the good
people who send their good works to assist in the royal
children's education and 'to cause important truths to be

instilled in their minds. *The lady's letter rather smells of the Bishop of Oxford.*"

Samuel, little as he was fitted to take the lead in thrashing out obscure theological subtleties, was, as the head of an important diocese and as a public man, an unqualified success. He served the Church well in the House of Lords. It was he who restored Convocation to life and usefulness, recovering for it all its ancient privileges which had lain dormant for more than a century. The Church, too, has reason to be grateful to him for scotching the Evangelical Lord Shaftesbury's foolish Bill for making the fifty-eighth Canon the final authority with regard to the use of ornaments, vestments and ritual (thus disregarding tradition, the discretion of the Bishops and the rights of congregations). Instead, he succeeded in having a Commission set up, himself sitting on it and drawing up the report—a report so thoroughly "Samwellian" that neither party was able to gain the upper hand.

On the divorce question he was as intolerant as his brethren on the Bench of Bishops, trying hard to introduce an amendment in the Divorce and Matrimonial Causes Bill of 1856—finally passed the following year—prohibiting the guilty parties to re-marry.

Why are bishops so adamant in their desire to condemn these ill-matched couples to life-long misery, and—if they manage to get a divorce and re-marry hoping for better luck —why do they refuse them the consolations of Book and Bell? Is there a special department run by Providence, that furnishes bishops with perfect spouses, thereby rendering them oblivious to the fact that such "little heavens below" are not universal outside the Episcopal Palace? It would seem so, and yet . . . one calls to mind Mrs. Proudie. The wife of a bishop, too, being only human and not so indifferent to earthly distinctions as is, of course, the lord of her bosom, must at times feel slightly irritated at hearing him addressed as "My Lord" by the world at large, while she, poor thing, remains plain—*sometimes very plain*—Mrs. Jones. And one seems to remember those among the rank and file of the clergy who would bear separation from their lawful ladies with more than Christian resignation; rather, let us say, with holy joy.

Samuel never forgot his father's advice to practise hospitality; not that he needed such advice, being naturally one of the kindest and most hospitable of men—lavish and generous to a fault. He was addicted to the barbarous custom of giving breakfasts; a custom that continued in vogue during more than half of the nineteenth century. The fashionable literary clubs had fixed days for breakfasts as well as for dinners, and many famous writers gave them in their own houses: those of Macaulay at his Chambers in Albany were very popular. Fancy Macaulay at breakfast! Reason staggers on its throne at the thought of that flood of eloquence and omniscience pouring forth with the coffee and ruthlessly annihilating any obstacle that tried to dam its course. The diary of Lord Carlisle contains many entries of these fearsome feasts. One of them reads: "Breakfast with the Bishop of Oxford, Hallam, Macaulay, Milan, Milnes. Extremely agreeable, and would have been still more so but there was a tendency to talk very loud and all at once." Another entry says: "The Bishop and I fought a mesmeric electro-biological battle against the scornful opposition of all the rest."

Certainly our grandfathers must have had remarkably sound constitutions to be able to stand the port wine they drank at night in those days and then cope with Macaulay at breakfast! Samuel, however, loved the custom and found it an excellent means of getting hold of people whom he had to consult about his innumerable activities. These activities, notwithstanding their varied nature, seldom led to unpleasantness with anyone. Twice, however, he came into conflict with Lord Westbury, when the latter was Lord Chancellor. The first occasion was during the debate on the Missionary Bishops' Bill. Lord Westbury said that it was in contravention to statute 25 Henry VIII which placed the crown as head of the Church. Samuel objected, saying: "The supremacy of the Crown is the supremacy of the law, but the law has never said that the Crown has the spiritual power of a bishop." To this Lord Westbury replied: "It is contended that I have made a mistake as to the word 'Spiritual'. Now, what is the oath of allegiance? It declares that no foreign prince, prelate, etc., hath, or ought to have, any jurisdiction, power, pre-eminence, or authority, civil or ecclesiastical, in this realm." And as to the Queen: "She is in all causes and in all matters within her dominions, supreme."

He had delivered himself to Samuel, who had an uncanny memory. "That," he said, "is another of those inaccuracies of statement of which I have to complain in so high a legal authority"; and he pointed out that the correct version was "in all causes and over all *persons* within these her dominions, supreme". "The *inaccurate* quotation," he went on to say, "marks what the noble Lord *wants and cannot find*, to establish his statement." As an ex-Lord Chancellor, meeting Samuel the next day, said: "I should think this morning Westbury feels the same sensation mentally that an Eton boy would bodily after an interview with Keate."

Lord Westbury did not forget this devastating snub, and on another occasion he tried to get his own back, describing a decision of the Bishop in Convocation as "a series of well-lubricated terms; a sentence so oily and saponaceous (doubtless a veiled allusion to Samuel's nickname) that no one can grasp it: like an eel it slips through your fingers and is simply nothing." He gained nothing by his personal abuse of Samuel who made a dignified and crushing reply. Members of the House of Lords were not then in the habit of indulging in personalities and did not like them. It was a long time before relations were resumed between them, and Lord Westbury took the first step. One day they met in the lobby of the House, and he held out his hand to Samuel, saying: "My Lord Bishop, as a Christian and a Bishop you will not refuse to shake hands." He went on: "Do you remember where we last met?" "No," said Samuel. "It was in the hour of my humiliation," replied Westbury, "when I was leaving the Queen's closet, after having given up the Great Seal. I met you on the stairs as I was coming out, and I felt inclined to say: 'Hast thou found me, Oh, mine enemy?'" Samuel was magnanimous enough not to remind him of the prophet's reply to Ahab's greeting! After Lord Westbury's death a mock epitaph on him, attributed to Sir Philip Rose, went the round of the clubs.

RICHARD, BARON WESTBURY
Lord High Chancellor of England.
He was an eminent Christian,
An energetic and merciful Statesman,
And a still more eminent and merciful Judge.
During his three years' tenure of office
He abolished the ancient method of
    conveying land,
The time-honoured institution of the
    Insolvents' Court.
    And
The eternity of Punishment.
Towards the close of his earthly career
In the Judicial Court of the Privy Council,
He dismissed Hell with costs,
And took away from orthodox members of the
    Church of England
Their last hope of Everlasting Damnation.

As time went on, Samuel's failure to cope adequately with the Oxford Movement, and his mishandling of the Hampden affair, were forgotten. After 1850 the Tractarian excitement died down; and "Hampden affairs" are fortunately rare. In the pulpit Samuel's popularity had never waned, and, as we have seen, he was a first-class administrator, handling his clergy and the organizations of his diocese with consummate tact and skill. He even earned the gratitude of Dr. Pusey and—of all things—through that white elephant of the Church, the Athanasian Creed!

The third Ritual Commission, held in 1871, had

recommended certain changes in it in order to make it somewhat less ferocious. Now—despite Lord Westbury— Churchmen of all shades of opinion refused indignantly to be jockeyed out of their hereditary right to go to Hell! Petitions protesting against any alteration of its dreary dogmas poured in. Pusey and Liddon, discreetly ignoring their disapproval of some of his past tactics, agreed that Samuel's powerful influence in high places must at all costs be enlisted in favour of St. Athanasius and wrote begging him to intervene. Pusey threatened to resign his living were one word of the Creed to be altered, and undoubtedly a large number of his followers would have done likewise. The Archbishop of Canterbury, having more confidence in the essential kindliness of the Almighty, was in favour of the changes.

"He's a Good Fellow, and 'twill all be well," he thought. Samuel, however, though he had too much sense of humour to take the intransigent Saint Athanasius very seriously and would have been quite willing to pour a little cold water on the fire and brimstone, persuaded His Grace that on no account must the Creed be touched. His counsel prevailed; to the joy of Pusey, who wrote to him: "Thanks be to God, and under God, and bless Him for Your Lordship's interposition." Bright[1] said: "Then the Church of England is saved. It is a heavy weight rolled off, after which one can breathe again freely."

Victoria, after the death of Albert, took Samuel back into favour. In 1873 she asked him to write an article in

[1]The then Regius Professor of Divinity at Oxford.

the *Quarterly Review* on the "Early Years of the Prince Consort"; and he preached at Osborne. We read in his diary: "After luncheon Queen saw me: very unusually kind, long talk. Spoke warmly about sermon, Prince of Wales, herself, Athanasian Creed, shortened services. I spoke warmly out on all, and she never so ready to listen, and seeming not hostile to any view of truth." His style in his diary is curiously reminiscent of Mr. Jingle.

There is not a shadow of evidence to support the opinion held by so many people—among them Albert and Greville—that Samuel used his high position and powerful influence for his own personal advantage. When in 1862 his great friend Dr. Sumner, the Archbishop of Canterbury, died, he wrote at once to Gladstone, suggesting Dr. Longley, the Archbishop of York, as the most fitting person to succeed him. The appointment was made, and Gladstone wrote to Palmerston warmly recommending Samuel for the Archbishopric of York. But in 1862 Albert though being dead yet spoke and the Bishop of London was given the Northern Primacy. That Samuel was not offered the See of London was owing to that wily Jew, Disraeli. The General Election on which his Ministry depended was going on, and he had been told that Samuel was a High Churchman. So, fearing to estrange the Evangelical vote, he passed him over. It was characteristic of his questionable methods. Samuel was of all the Bishops the most suitable for the post, and it was universally expected that it would be offered to him. The Dean of Windsor wrote him: "Disraeli has been utterly ignorant, utterly unprincipled; he rode the

Protestant horse one day, then got frightened that it had gone too far and was injuring the county elections, so he went right round and proposed names never heard of. Nothing he would not have done, but throughout he was most hostile to you: he alone prevented London being offered you."

Samuel was translated to Winchester, where he had already held a Canonry, in 1869, his friend Gladstone consulting him before naming him to the Queen. It was not a very advantageous exchange, the upkeep of the Palace being so expensive. The corridors alone require no less than three miles of carpet. The work, too, was far harder, and the diocese needed to be reorganized. But Samuel was attached to Hampshire, in which County he had first worked first as country parson and archdeacon and then as Canon.

CHAPTER FOUR

SAMUEL was not only a hard worker himself: he had the faculty of making other people work for him and getting the best out of them. It was sometimes a doubtful pleasure to be invited to Cuddesdon. "After breakfast"—Dean Burgon tells us—"he retired to his library requesting the Archdeacons, Chaplains and Clergy to follow him speedily, so that long before eleven they had plunged *in medias res*—the business (whatever it was) that had brought them all up to Cuddesdon. At the end of two or three hours of application most of those present had slipped away for luncheon and again returned to sit in conclave. Wilberforce alone could never be persuaded to stir. I once brought him a biscuit and a glass of sherry. He thanked me for my zeal, laughing; but was inexorable. He "never did" and was "better without it". The long summer afternoon wore away, and the room at last grew oppressively close. At five o'clock nods and winks indicative of exhaustion were freely interchanged, but no one moved—the chief personage having as yet shown no signs of fatigue.

At length the clock struck six, and "I say!"—exclaimed some bold spirit—"I have got the cramp and must go for a walk." The standard of rebellion once set up, the room began to clear. "Well then," the Bishop would say, "we had better break off, for I see some of you are getting tired."

So satisfactory a recognition of the fact produced a general rising, and a pleasant vision floated before each one's eyes of a rush through the sweet evening air before having to dress for dinner. Vain dream! "My dear Randall, *you* are not leaving us, are you?" The good old man murmured something about "not minding stopping". This act of self-sacrifice was so gratefully acknowledged that it was quite impossible for "My dear Clarke" or "My dear Bickersteth" or "My dear anyone else" to decline, as the Bishop challenged us severally to do him the great favour to stay and help him with his post. In this way he secured the services of a dozen white negroes, whom he overwhelmed with thanks and writing materials.

"Now then, are you ready?" (throwing a letter across to "My dear Woodford") "Begin, 'My dear Sir' and finish 'Yours truly' say 'I shall be glad to confirm at your Church on the day and at the hour you propose'." "Will you," turning to the man on his left and handing him a letter, "explain to him that I cannot possibly sanction what would be a grave irregularity, but that," etc., etc. "Thank you, my dear Pearson." To the next scribe, "Begin 'My dear Mrs. S.' (naming her) 'Yes, we all grow older. Thank you much for your photograph. I enclose you in return what you are good enough to ask for'." To the next "Dear Sir, the last sherry was excellent. I shall be glad if you will send me a further supply of precisely the same quality at the same price." In this way perhaps forty or fifty letters were written and it was already past seven. All were again thanked and invited to dress for dinner. Some gentry of the neighbourhood had been asked to meet them. Samuel had been at work since breakfast and looked tired out, but there was still "a little thing he *must* do" before he could go to dress. But at dinner he looked ten years younger and was the life and soul of the party, eating and drinking freely, telling amusing stories and looking after everyone.

Society acted on him like a stimulant, and he loved it. Fashionable ladies vied with each other to get him to dine with them, and invitations from all the great country houses, including Sandringham, were showered upon him.

He was very quick-witted. A conversation arose after dinner as to the difficulty of rendering some English words into Latin. "You cannot put 'hearse' into Latin," said one of the guests. "Oh, that is easy enough," said Samuel: *"Mors omnibus"*.

Another time the word drysalter cropped up, and a lady asked: "What is a drysalter?" "Tait and Bradley!"[1] answered Samuel. "My dear Clarke," he said one day to the Archdeacon of Oxford, "tell me why an archdeacon's apron is like unwholesome food?" On being asked for the answer he replied: "Because it goes against his stomach."

Children he adored. At a conference of Sunday School teachers he said that it was a "mistaken idea to take children whom God had made volatile, who could not be still for a moment, because it was their nature, who were always dropping off to sleep on the benches they sat on because they needed sleep, and would begin to whisper and laugh to one another because they needed that sort of thing just as

---

[1]Tait and Bradley's metrical version of the Psalms.

much as the bee needed to go buz-uz when he flies about—
to take little creatures made in this way, to sit them on a
hard bench, to make horrid faces at them when they began
to buzz or knock them on the head if they went to sleep"
was fatal. He told them that the "be good, be good, be
good" system was a failure, and that the only way to win
children was to love them, make them happy, and to expect
very little from them. *Punch* made this speech the subject
of a cartoon entitled: "Wilberforce Secundus Emancipating
the poor little Whites". Up to the time of his death he
worked as hard as he had ever worked. He would have
had little sympathy with the Levites of whom we are told
in the Bible—"and from the age of fifty years they shall
cease waiting upon the service thereof (the Tabernacle) and
shall serve no more".

On July 19th 1873, when he was riding with Lord
Granville to lunch at the house of Mr., afterwards
Lord Farrar, death stopped the way. His horse put
its foot into a hole in the turf and stumbled, throwing him
so violently that his death was practically instantaneous. It
was one of fate's curious ironies that this practised horseman,
who had ridden all his life, should meet his end in this
manner, particularly as he had just been joking over the
horsemanship of one of his friends, a distinguished political
peer. A psychic guest at the house at which he was
expected saw him at the exact moment of the accident and
cried out: "Here is the Bishop."

Perhaps there was no more sincerely religious man in
England than Samuel Wilberforce. He caused to be

inscribed on the screen of the private Chapel in his Palace:
"We Will Give Ourselves Continually to Prayer and to the
Ministry of the Word". He lived up to this motto to the
best of his ability; indeed, his inner spiritual life was far
deeper than most people suspected. He was intensely sympathetic, large-hearted and generous and always eager to enter
into the difficulties and sorrows of his fellow men and to
help them. But his character was not a deep one. Life, as
in the case of Mendelssohn, had been too easy for him,
preferment too rapid, the world too much at his feet, and
his natural charm and amiability had made his path still
smoother. He was so sure of himself, so fertile in
expedients, so persuasive, that he gave cause to the many
who considered him insincere—which he was not. And,
as we have seen, his *facile* easy going nature made him trust
other people too easily, and he was often obliged to revoke
his decisions and retract his words.

Samuel was the first to die of those three fortunate
youths who were friends together at Oriel. Success,
such as comes to few of us, was the lot of all three.
To which of them did that success bring the greatest
happiness? Surely not to the hard bitter Cardinal,
trampling relentlessly underfoot everybody and everything
that stood in the way of his ambition. Nor to the unctuous
self-righteous wily politician "drunk with the exuberance
of his own verbosity". Rather, it seems, to the kindly
humane Bishop . . . Soapy Sam. Yes, but there are worse
things than soap: Vinegar, for instance!

To have journeyed through life winning people instead

of antagonizing them: saying kind words—doing kind actions. Making life a little brighter to the human shadows with whom we come in contact e'er our "brief candle" be snuffed out by the great Extinguisher is perhaps to have lived not unworthily. And, after all, the sterner virtues are not the only ones that may be accounted unto a man for righteousness.

"God fulfils Himself in many ways".

HARRIET MARTINEAU

VIRTUE IS ITS OWN REWARD
(Harriet Martineau)

CHAPTER ONE

"All propagated with the Best Intentions."

BYRON (*Don Juan*)

IT is given to few (except the very young) to have reached absolute certainty concerning every question that perplexes humanity; to still fewer to have succeeded in inducing a large number of our fellow creatures to believe in our omniscience. Yet such was the happy state of that amazing person, Harriet Martineau, whose name was for many years a household word in England. Cabinet Ministers sought her opinion with regard to political matters: Society lionized her; and publishers, magazines and newspapers competed for the books, articles and pamphlets on every conceivable subject, which she poured forth in a never-ending stream. With one exception, they are all now as dead as the hand that penned them. The exception is her "Autobiography". It is a remarkable work—almost modern in its self-revelation and worship of the scientific outlook—yet, in its intense egoism and priggishness, wholly of its period; a period in which everything, good and bad, was done from the highest motives and in which the tolerant self-doubting disillusioned spirit of to-day was unborn.

Harriet was born at Norwich in 1802. Her father was

a pillar of that strange sect, the Unitarians, and she was the sixth of a family of eight. They were brought up with all the strictness of a provincial dissenting family in the days when parents were benevolent autocrats whose lightest word had all the authority of the laws and the prophets.

Harriet was a delicate neurotic child, and indigestion made life a misery to her—especially at night. She tells us how the dim light from the window seemed to advance and bear down on her eyeballs until it threatened to crush them; how savage beasts chased her, and how she dreamed of standing in a cold sweat at the head of the staircase not daring to move for fear of the abyss beneath. Her panics were hardly less in her waking hours. Such was her terror of a magic lantern that the first sight of the white circle and the moving slides always brought on diarrhœa—to her intolerable shame. An uncomfortable child with, as she herself describes it, a "hellish temper": the family remedy was milk. A hundred years ago it was not the fashion to study children's temperaments and idiosyncrasies; there was a nursery code and they must conform to it. Milk was good for children, so they must drink it; and, if it made them sick, it was certainly due to some strange moral perversity on their part. Then, too, Harriet was born entirely without the sense of smell and with very little sense of taste, so she was cut off from one of the greatest joys of childhood and, for many, *the* greatest solace of old age!

It was, as might be expected, an intensely religious household. Though Unitarians (one gathers) do not believe in hell, heaven was taken quite literally, and so enticing was its prospect to this unhappy child that she frequently planned suicide in order to reach it sooner. One day she even went to the kitchen to get a carving-knife with which to cut her throat but—finding the servants at dinner—did not like to deprive them of it. She imagined heaven as a place gay with yellow and lilac crocuses—a more seductive vision of the celestial regions than that of the pearly gates, golden floor, and milk and honey diet given us in the popular hymns we used to sing so ecstatically. But, of course, such a *régime* would not have tempted the bilious Harriet. This material view of heaven exists even now. There is a quite recent devotional book called "The Delightful Joys of Heaven",[1] which tells us seriously that the designs of the Altar, the tabernacle and various other Church furnishings are still in use there. We are also informed that, as it has a government, politicians will find scope for their nefarious activities; though here we cannot help thinking the author is perhaps a little too optimistic. She—the book is, of course, written by a lady—tells us that composers of music will be much in request, but that their talents will be utilized solely in writing masses for very large forces—the whole Company of the Blessed, in fact, accompanied by the heavenly orchestra. It is pleasant to know that literature is one of the "Delightful Joys". The "Autobiography of St. Peter" should be at least as interesting as that of Miss Martineau, and the "Reminiscences of Lucifer"—specially bound and insured against fire—would doubtless be a "best seller"!

---

[1]"Society for the Promotion of Christian Knowledge."

From earliest childhood Harriet was obsessed with religion. She wrote sermons almost as soon as she had learnt how to write, and at nine years old asked her brother Thomas—aged nineteen—to explain why, if God foreknew everything, we should be rewarded or punished for actions already settled in advance. Thomas, curiously enough, was unable to solve the problem satisfactorily. The Trinity did not puzzle her. She had heard it defined as "mere nonsense" by the minister of the chapel they attended. "Here," said he, taking three wine glasses and placing them in a row, "here is the Father—here's the Son—and here's the Holy Ghost: do you mean to tell me that those three glasses can in any case be one?" And that was that! But the questions of foreknowledge and free will continued to cry for solution, more especially as she had read in Milton—the first poet she had managed to get hold of—that they were favourite topics in hell.

It must have been a strange household. The mother was a hard, clever, managing woman with social ambitions —a petty tragedy, this. To be the wife of a dissenter in a Cathedral City and to have social ambitions! But, oddly enough, she did not share the current opinion that needlework and domestic affairs were the only occupations suitable for her sex: she considered that women were as well able as men to profit by education. So, although the girls sewed, ironed, mended, made their own clothes and learnt to cook and do all the things that were done at home in those days, they also studied seriously. Thomas—whose theology had so disappointed Harriet—taught them Latin; Sister Rachel,

French and English, and Henry, the second brother, arithmetic. Henry, an unregenerate youth, was apt to take his sisters and their lessons as a joke—to the great annoyance of Harriet—a portentously serious child, who, throughout her life, was joke-proof. Poor Henry; he was only fifteen: One rather likes the glimpse one gets of him. Music was taught them by Mr. Beckwith, the organist of the Cathedral. Harriet was fond of music. As she herself modestly tells us, she was never known to sing out of tune, and "There was no music that I ever attempted that I did not understand and could not execute—under the one indispensable condition, *that nobody heard me.*" As it is unfortunately difficult to conquer the technical difficulties of music without being heard—at any rate by one's teacher—her lessons did not yield the result that might have been attained by a less retiring pupil. "Heaven opened before me at the sound of my own voice when I believed myself alone," says Harriet. She was certainly not an engaging child; but probably many of her defects were due to shyness. "I had an unbounded need of approbation and affection," she writes. So, as she could not command it from others, she bestowed it on herself in full meed.

When Harriet was eleven a great event occurred: She was sent to school. The school was kept by a Mr. Perry, who had been Minister of an orthodox dissenting chapel, but who became converted to Unitarianism. "Strange that such difference should be!" and unfortunate for Mr. Perry, as he lost not only his pulpit but most of his pupils and was obliged to supplement his diminished numbers by taking girls. He was born to teach them, says Harriet, being gentlemanly and honourable but far too easily imposed on to teach boys. The girls sat at the front desks and could not see the boys except by looking round. Their necks must have become permanently twisted. Small, however, as was Harriet's opinion of boys, she was impressed by the thorough way in which they did their lessons. It was the only time in her life that she realized the superiority of the male sex. One day, when Mr. Perry was called out of the room, the little ruffians would not let the girls work. They made faces, bow-wowed, bleated and made ribald cheeky remarks in the immemorial manner of boyhood. Naturally the girls, after *their* manner, decided that Mr. Perry must be told, and Harriet accepted the *rôle* of tale-bearer. It did not add to her popularity. One is glad to learn that she felt some qualms of conscience at seeing the unfortunate youngsters kept in to learn endless lines of Greek.

But, when it came to studying, Harriet was all there. Cicero, Virgil and a little Horace were her chief reading, and she took, before long, a great delight in Tacitus: She even *thought* in Latin. Her master gave her a translation of some verses from the Æneid to turn back into the original, and lo! her version was, with the exception of one word, exactly the same as that of Virgil himself! Mathematics were to her a plaything, and composition a labour of love. She varied her studies by writing little tracts and religious exercises. She was also extremely fond of reading the newspaper and had her own opinions with regard to the National Debt and political economy in general. But, notwithstand-

ing the pleasure she derived from her studies, she remained
un enfant de misère—misunderstood, unhealthy and, worst
of all, deaf. The deafness began when she was about twelve
and increased alarmingly. It made her a sore trial to her
family, who insisted on ignoring it and accused her of not
listening when they spoke to her. Perhaps there are few
greater afflictions than deafness, and none that make social
relations more difficult—and Harriet's family life was
already difficult enough in all conscience. Finally, unable
to stand her temper and depressions any longer, they sent
her to a school in Bristol kept by an aunt.

It was a great relief to everyone concerned. The aunt
and cousins were clever and sympathetic, and Harriet
responded to their kindness. Their thirst for knowledge
was appalling. Says Harriet: "I still think that I have never
met with a family to compare with theirs for power of
acquisition or effective use of knowledge. They would learn
a new language at odd moments; get through a tough
philosophical book by taking turns in the Court for air;
write down an entire lecture or sermon without missing a
sentence; get round the piano after a concert and play and
sing over every new piece that had been performed." A
truly remarkable family!

She returned to Norwich in 1819 much improved,
though still, apparently, none too amiable. Her relations
with her mother became less strained, but she quarrelled
with her younger brother James to whom she had been
intensely devoted. The least satisfactory of all human
affections, she tells us, is the fraternal. It is quite natural;

brothers and sisters are rarely on equal terms. In all well regulated families boys are regarded as superior beings, and their sisters are quite content to yield them first place—giving way to and adoring the delightful creatures. The exacting morose Harriet must have been extraordinarily difficult to get on with, and James seems to have had a strong and attractive personality. Harriet hints that " 'an she would" she could a tale unfold, but she refrains from telling it. She always regretted the breach.

> "To be wroth with one we love
> Doth work like madness in the brain."

At this time she was *desperately* religious; a mournful fanatical superstitious religion. Hour after hour she pored over the Bible, reading every commentary and religious work she could get hold of; but already doubts had begun to stir in her mind. She felt the need of *"a clear distinction between the knowable and the unknowable"*—dangerous ground for the Christian to venture on! "Where shall wisdom be found? and where is the place of understanding?" The search has passionately interested man since the dawn of his human consciousness—but to no avail. God refuses to reveal His secret, and man is forced to the conclusion that, unless Faith steps in where Knowledge ceases, no dogmatic creed can serve him. And faith is not to be acquired by study. It is a gift; just as much as is the genius of a Bach or a Chopin. Perhaps the believer may retort: "But what about St. Paul or St. Augustine? They did not start as believers." True; but the capacity for faith was there—undeveloped or working in another direction.

Harriet's preoccupation with religious matters occasioned her *début* as a writer. She wrote an article called "Female Writers on Practical Divinity" which she signed "V" and sent to *The Monthly Repository*, an obscure Unitarian publication. In fear and trembling she waited for the next number, and, when with beating heart she opened it, there was her article and (in the notices to correspondents) a request to hear more of "V". One memorable day she went to tea with her beloved Thomas and his newly wedded wife. Thomas had the *Repository* and began reading her contribution. "Ah! this is a new hand; they have had nothing so good as this for a long time," said he. "What a fine sentence this is! Why, do you not think so?" She mumbled untruthfully that she did not think much of it. "Then you were not listening; I will read it again." With many blushes Harriet at length acknowledged that she was the author and was rewarded by Thomas saying to her: "Now, dear, leave it to others to make shirts and darn stockings, and do you devote yourself to this."

From now on nothing, of course, could stop her. She wrote a book, "Devotional Exercises"—which Thomas did *not* like—and then began a sort of theological-metaphysical novel, which was to enlighten the world on this light and popular subject. Alas! when she had written half the first volume even Harriet herself had to acknowledge that it was so excessively dull that nobody would be likely to read it. She had already decided on her method of authorship and had made the discovery that it was a waste of time to copy what she wrote. Especially did she dislike Miss Edgeworth's practice of revising her novels, changing passages and submitting the manuscripts to her father before publication. She looked at her work and saw that it was good and that, if she altered anything, she was always obliged to change it back to its original form. Such is Inspiration. Hers was not the method of Anatole France who once told the writer that he frequently re-wrote whole chapters four or five times. His style, however, does not resemble that of Harriet.

. . . . .

"Sweet are the uses of adversity!" Harriet learnt this valuable truth through a long series of calamities. By the time she was twenty, her deafness had become a serious obstacle to her intercourse with others. Vanity prevented her using a trumpet; (indeed, she did not take to one for ten years) so people shunned her—which naturally increased her already abnormal morbidity and self-consciousness. Then her brother Thomas—the one member of her family with whom she got on—developed consumption. He went to Madeira for the climate but died on his way home, his baby boy having died soon after their arrival in Madeira. Next came the decline of her father's fortunes. In 1824, the last year of his prosperity, he gave Harriet and Henry the money to go for a walking tour in Scotland. They walked five hundred miles in a month, and the fatigue and rough food had a deplorable effect on Harriet's weak stomach. To walk five hundred miles in Scotland in 1824 must have needed considerable courage. It is to be hoped that Henry was more sympathetic about her digestion than he was over the arithmetic lessons. It was their last extravagance; their father was involved in the financial collapse of 1826 and died shortly afterwards much impoverished. His last days were consoled by Harriet's "Devotional Exercises".

But worse remained behind: she lost her chance of getting married. If she gives a correct impression of her own personality at this period, it is difficult to imagine that she ever had a lover. Be that as it may, there was certainly a poor but virtuous Mr. Worthington, who had hitherto hesitated to ask her to share his poverty. When evil days came upon her family, he nobly came forward, but, sad to relate, the sudden prospect of being united to Harriet was too much for him. He became insane! The trouble was aggravated by the behaviour of Mr. Worthington's family who—she tells us—actually and incredibly believed that she was engaged to another young man at the same time. In the biography she writes: "There has never been any doubt in my mind that, considering what I was in those days, it was happiest for us both that our union was prevented by any means." Never, she goes on to say, did she ever suffer from the pangs of love or the desire to be married. The older she grew the more "serious and irremediable" seemed to her the evils and disadvantages of married life.

During all these troubles she continued to write— mournful poems and religious tracts all about death and damnation, for which she received a pound a piece. They were published by a solemn old Calvinistic publisher in Shropshire—gloomy and pessimistic as "Shropshire Lads" are wont to be! He suggested that she should write short stories, so she wrote a gay trifle called "The Rioters", following it up with one on "Wages" and another called "Principle and Practice". About this time she came across Mrs. Marcet's "Conversations on Political Economy" and, on reading it, discovered that she had nothing to learn on the subject. But her chief stand-by was still *The Repository*. It had a new editor, a Mr. Fox, who begged her to contribute. She *did* : essays, reviews and poetry flowed from her relentless pen, and, though payment was slow and poor, the experience was valuable.

Misfortune was still dogging the family : its last blow was the failure of the business in which the greater part of the remnant of her father's fortune was invested; so Harriet had to support herself. Fortunately the family house was still theirs. For two years she lived on about fifty pounds a year, chiefly earned by her skill with the needle. Perhaps it was a good thing for her in the long run, for it certainly helped her to conquer the morbid shyness caused by her deafness and bad health. Religion, once more, came to her aid—not exactly in the accepted manner, but in a more practical sense.

The Unitarian Association conceived the happy idea of offering prizes for the three essays which should present the charms of their creed most alluringly to Roman Catholics, Jews and Mohammedans. The prizes were respectively ten, fifteen and twenty guineas. A more sophisticated Society might possibly have devoted the first prize to the conversion of the Roman Catholics. Jews are often better Christians than the Christians themselves, and Turks and infidels are not numerous in England. The spectacle of the Pope renouncing both the heresies of Rome and the triple tiara and leading the singing at St. Peter's— converted into a Unitarian Chapel—while the College of Cardinals acted as Elders would be a highly edifying one. But still, to convert the countless hordes of *Islam* to Unitarianism would be a triumph indeed! To see the lordly Arab forsaking his *burnous* and his *mosque* and going to Chapel in a top hat; to cause the gentle Turk to give up his national pastime—the massacre of Armenians—and employ his leisure hours reading the prize essay! It was worth twenty guineas. Harriet, who would cheerfully have advocated even Christian Science—had it then been invented—for a fiver, decided to go in for all three prizes. Her method was simple. She borrowed all the books she could find on the three religions, swotted them up, embodied the results in her essays—and won all three prizes! Unfortunately the Unitarian Association neglected to publish a list of the resultant conversions. The reading Harriet did for the Jewish essay inspired her with "the Hope of the Hebrew" (Was the Hope Unitarianism?), the study of Catholicism with an essay on Baptism, and Unitarianism itself with "An Early Sowing".

But, since Harriet had read Mrs. Marcet's "Conversations", political Economy had filled her mind. It was not, she was forced to admit, a subject that had much appeal for the masses; but why not *make* it appealing? As she read Mrs. Marcet's exciting pages, characters illustrating the various Economic principles rose up from them. *She* could give profit and loss all the glamour of fiction. Under *her* pen the working of the Poor Law would be as exciting as a really good murder story. "I mentioned my notion," she tells us, "when we were sitting at work one bright afternoon at home. Brother James nodded assent: my mother said: 'Do it,' and we went to tea unconscious what a great thing we had done since dinner."

CHAPTER TWO

IF the prize essay did not result in the immediate conversion of the world to Unitarianism, at least the forty-five pounds gave Harriet a breathing-space in which to think out the Political Economy Series (she always refers to it in capitals) which was to achieve the almost equally remarkable feat of, as she tells us, "assisting the poor to manage their own welfare." No wonder she felt at first overwhelmed by the magnitude of the undertaking—"the strongest effort of will that I ever committed myself to". But Harriet was nothing if not public-spirited, and the thought of the toiling multitudes who "needed"—nay *"craved"* for—the "Series" gave her courage. Faith, she knew, moved mountains, and so she formed certain resolutions from which she promised herself no power on earth should draw her away. "I was resolved that, in the first place, the thing should be done. The people wanted the book and they should have it." She also resolved that she would sustain her health until the economic salvation of England was assured; that she would never lose her temper—perhaps, for Harriet, the most difficult to keep of all her resolutions. She knew she was right, "and people who are aware that they are in the right need *never* lose temper"! Lastly she decided not to borrow any money from her family.

Obviously the first thing to do was to find a publisher,

which was not easy. She wrote to several, but they all with one consent excused themselves—"It was a bad year"; "the bishops had just thrown out the Reform Bill"; "there was the cholera scare". Messrs. Baldwin and Craddock, however, asked her to call on them. She did so on her way back from Dublin, where she had gone to visit her brother James, taking a lawyer cousin as a witness. Messrs. Baldwin and Craddock sat superb in their arm-chairs, bewigged and cautious, and made objections after the manner of publishers. Messrs. Baldwin and Craddock also urged the Reform Bill and the Cholera and dared to suggest that the words "Political Economy" should be omitted in the title. Great was Harriet's indignation at this sacrilegious proposal; but Messrs. Baldwin and Craddock were unmoved. "With heartless guile they dallied awhile", as the song says, and threw their chance away. With sighs and tears poor Harriet returned to Norwich and wrote to one publisher after another, receiving instant refusals from all but one firm, Messrs. Whitaker, who offered to do their best for the "Series" while requiring her to guarantee them against loss. What should she do? "Go to London," said Henry; so to London she went by coach on a miserable December day, inviting herself to stay with a cousin who owned a large brewery in Shoreditch.

Armed with a letter from Mr. Fox, the editor of the *Repository*, she presented herself the following morning to another publisher. Again polite refusals: the Reform Bill and the Cholera. Day after day of that cold foggy December it was the same dreary story, and night after night she sat

up writing the even more dreary opening numbers of the
"Series". Then one morning Mr. Fox, who had a brother
in London named Charles who kept a bookshop, gave her
a folded paper saying that he was ashamed to ask her to
read it, but that it would at least enable her to go to a good
publisher and say that she had had an offer. She went back
to Mr. Whitaker who received her very rudely and again
refused to entertain the idea. So in despair she considered
Charles Fox's proposition: it was not encouraging. It
stipulated that the "Series" must be published by subscription and that the subscription must be for five hundred
copies in advance; that subscribers should be guaranteed by
both parties, and that Fox was to have half the profits besides
the usual bookseller's commission and privileges. It was
rather a one-sided bargain. Fox had neither money nor
influence—he never procured a single subscriber—and in
case of failure he stood to lose nothing. Harriet says some
rather hard things about him, but, after all, he was only
protecting his own interests. She disliked the idea of
bringing out her book privately; it was a terrible blow to
her self-esteem, and the contemptuous letters she received
when she appealed for subscriptions humiliated her still
more. But it was her only chance, so she drew up a
prospectus and submitted it to her friend Mr. Fox. She
found him in a pessimistic mood. He had spoken to James
Stuart Mill who thought little of her idea—still less, probably, of her capacity to carry it out. She saw her last
opportunity slipping away and said: "If you wish that your
brother should draw back, say so now. Here is the

advertisement. Make up your mind before it goes to press."
He said he did not wish to give up the idea altogether.
"Yes, you do," replied Harriet; "but I tell you this—the
people want this book, and they *shall* have it." In the end
she had to accept fresh terms; that, if, when two numbers
had been published, the subscriptions had not reached a
thousand, the publication should cease.

It would be a mistake to suppose that Harriet was not
entirely convinced that the whole of England was not
groaning in a bondage from which only that *manna* from
heaven—her "Series"—could release it. She had unbounded
confidence in herself and an abysmal ignorance of human
nature, and not a gleam of humour lightened the portentous
seriousness of her character. But, although she herself
never guessed it, this little unattractive sickly and deaf
creature from Norwich was urged by a far more powerful
incentive than that of an all consuming zeal for the welfare
of humanity—an all consuming personal pride and ambition. She was, in truth, bursting with self-esteem, and,
when vanity, ambition and a boundless capacity for hard
work are combined with a passion for reforming other
people, something generally happens. And to the amaze-
ment of everyone concerned—except Harriet—something
did happen: the "Series" was a triumphant success! Everything went wrong at first. The weekly reports from Charles
Fox before the publication were gloomy in the extreme.
Subscriptions were not coming in; the booksellers were not
interested; it was foredoomed to failure he said. Perhaps
the clever suggestion of Harriet's mother that she should

send a letter puffing the book to every member of both Houses of Parliament had more to do with its immediate success than anything else. Within ten days Fox sold two thousand copies, and the sales finally exceeded five thousand.

Harriet had certainly "arrived". Publishers vied with one another to secure the rights of the "Series". Members of Parliament sent her blue books in such quantities that the local postmaster begged her to collect her own correspondence, and *real* London celebrities begged for the honour of her acquaintance. Norwich was now too small for Harriet. She must migrate to London.

It is difficult to account for the success of the "Series", for, truth to tell, the stories are quite unreadable nowadays. They consist of a mixture of elementary, borrowed, half-baked and undigested science served up in the form of dull fiction wholly without a redeeming feature. But she had chosen the right moment. Reform was in the air. The Reform Bill was the dominant political question; young Mr. Dickens was beginning to attack social abuses, and the demand for education was making itself heard. Almost any instructive writer would have been read, and, as most of the readers of the "Series" knew even less about Political Economy than did the author, there was no one except Mr. Mill to challenge her proud eminence as a Political Economist. Whether the toiling multitude—who were to find economic salvation through the "Series"—read, learnt and inwardly digested it is open to question. If they did, their digestions must have been stronger than that of the author herself. But in any case the toiling multitudes were now of less consequence; they had served their purpose. Harriet, who was not averse to appreciation in more exalted circles, gives us a touching picture of the little Princess Victoria "running and skipping to show her mother the advertisement of the Illustrations of Taxation and to get leave to order them. Her *favourite* of my stories is 'Ella of Garreloch' ". Of the "French Wine and Politics" an unkind writer said that it saved Harriet the trouble of assuring the public that she had never travelled in France.

.   .   .   .   .

And so to London Harriet went, settling herself in lodgings in Conduit Street. She at once became the fashion; but she did not allow her social engagements to interfere with her work. *"Things were pressing to be said, and I was the person to say them."* There was the "Series" to be completed, and she explains at great length her method of writing it, which, she frankly admits, was to get from the library every book she could discover concerning the particular number she happened to be writing and borrow her material, not troubling herself with any other branch of the subject until she needed to get it up. "Sufficient unto the day!" Such a method has its advantages, though it is, perhaps, hardly calculated to give a particularly comprehensive view of the subject as a whole.

Harriet worked every day from seven a.m. until two o'clock, when visitors began to arrive; then she went for a walk, returning to dress "before the carriage came—somebody's carriage being always sent—to take me out to dinner. An evening visit or two closed the day's engagements." She was accused of giving herself airs, as she did not return the visits she received, but, as she pointed out, she had no carriage and the fatigue would have been too great. Sydney Smith suggested that she could have got over the difficulty by sending round an inferior authoress in a carriage to drop the cards. If her head had been a little turned, it would not have been surprising. Yesterday she was poor and unknown, and to-day she found herself courted and flattered by Society and lulled into a self-complacency (even greater than that she already possessed) by the subtle incense which the most distinguished men of the day burnt at her shrine. But Harriet was quite unable to take the world as she found it and to enjoy her celebrity *sans arrière pensée*. Like most deaf people, she was suspicious and could not refrain from looking the gift horse in the mouth. She imagined she saw patronage in every overture made to her. When invited to Lansdowne House she declined to go, saying that she would go nowhere but where her acquaintance was sought "as a lady, by ladies". It was useless for Mr. Hallam to explain that Lady Lansdowne being one of the Queen's ladies, and Lord Lansdowne a Cabinet Minister, they could not make calls. Was she not Harriet Martineau, the author of the "Series"?

This attitude was, of course, merely another form of the snobbishness she criticized in others. She wanted to be loved for her own charms and could not understand that there was no earthly reason—apart from her notoriety —why people should want to make her acquaintance. She was poor and unattractive, and her deafness effectually prevented her from shining as a conversationalist; so what had she to offer in exchange for the hospitality she received? There is nothing more agreeable than a society in which the best of the various worlds meet—social, political, diplomatic, artistic and literary—but those who secure the *entrée* through their talents should be content to play the game as it is understood by the other players.

Harriet gives us an interesting picture of literary lionism in her day. She strongly disapproved of it. What *she* would have liked was the tribute paid to Petrarch when he mounted the steps of the Capitol crowned with laurel and preceded by twelve noble youths reciting his verses. "Literary lions," she tells us, "now constitute a class—the lady of the house devotes herself to 'drawing out' the guest, asks for her opinion of this, that and the other book and intercedes for her young friends, trembling on their chairs, that each may be favoured with 'just one line for her Album'. The children are kept in the nursery as being unworthy of the notice of a literary person, or brought up severally into the Presence, that they may have it to say all their lives that they had been introduced." Such scenes, she tells us, were very common in country-houses.

Harriet found it all very deplorable. Why should an author such as she was be obliged to submit to being gazed at in public? Why should she receive flattery as if it were welcome, when she would fain occupy herself with something far higher and better than herself and her doings? But then, one may ask, why need she accept Mrs. Leo

Hunter's invitation? The reason, one fears, is because—humiliating as it is to be appreciated—it is infinitely worse to be ignored! And no one would have disliked it more than Harriet herself.

In the meantime, the "Series" was earning golden opinions. Lord Brougham—who seems to have entertained an amused admiration for its author—suggested that she should write four extra numbers for the "Society for the Diffusion of Useful Knowledge" at the rate of one hundred pounds an article, the Society paying her three hundred and he himself the remaining hundred. The Society paid up, but Brougham did not. Harriet did not like him; she emphatically denied the report—so generally believed—that she had sought his patronage. All connection with the Whig Government and Lord Brougham she considered detrimental to her usefulness and influence: and she was convinced that that influence was likely to become a determining factor in European politics, for Louis Philippe ordered a copy of the "Series" for every member of his family. This was followed by a similar order from the Emperor of Russia; but alas! the references to the rights of the people did not please those exalted personages, and she was informed of the fact. The Emperor, indeed, ordered every copy to be delivered up and burnt and forbade her to enter his empire. His example was followed by Austria and Italy. Was it the matter or the manner of the "Series" that so offended Royalty? Could it possibly have bored Their Majesties? But Harriet was nothing daunted. She wrote for "the People", she said, and "crowned heads" must take their chance. Did not one know that press agents had not been invented in 1833, one would suspect Harriet of having had a very efficient one.

But even in England there were crumpled leaves in Harriet's bed of roses. The famous Lockhart of the *Quarterly Review*, oddly enough, did not admire the "Series". He said so; in fact, he wrote an extremely rude and, it must be admitted, quite indefensible article about it. Harriet read it on Good Friday, and such was the beauty of her character that when she went to bed she was able to say that the day had been a "very happy one". She writes: "The testing of one's endurance is pleasurable; and the testing of one's power of forgiveness is yet sweeter. . . . The compassion that I felt on this occasion for the low-minded and foul-mouthed creatures who could use their education and position as Gentlemen to 'destroy' a woman—was very painful." So she ignored the insult. Perhaps she realized that "silence is the unbearable repartee!" She tells us that the circulation of the "Series" increased largely after the appearance of Lockhart's article and diminished "markedly and immediately" on the publication of an extremely flattering one in the *Edinburgh Review*, though it is a little difficult to reconcile her statement with the fact that both articles appeared in the same month—April, 1835.

Apart from these small worries, all was going well. She wrote articles on domestic service for the Poor Law Commissioners—"The Maid of all Work", "The Housemaid" and "The Dressmaker"—"A Manchester Strike", for the operatives of that city—"The Life of a Salmon," probably for the Fishmongers' Company—and "What there is in a Button", doubtless for the Haberdashers. She planned pictures with David Wilkie. He discussed with her the incidents in the "Series" that he could use as subjects; indeed, so great was his admiration for those fascinating stories that nothing, he said, would make him so happy as to be able to spend the rest of his painting life "in making a gallery from my Series". After ten months in the Conduit Street lodgings, Harriet took a small house in Fludyer Street, Westminster, where she was joined by her mother and an aunt. The experiment was not very successful. Both mother and daughter had strong personalities, and Mrs. Martineau, who delighted in her new social sphere, intensely disliked playing second fiddle to Harriet. Besides which, she considered the house too small, the neighbourhood too humble. What was the use of knowing all these smart people if you did not keep up some sort of style? Harriet was quite right in insisting on living well within her means. Her rigid honesty was one of her best qualities, but her conscious moral rectitude and priggish self-complacency must have made her somewhat difficult to live with. One rather pities the two old ladies.

. . . . .

Not the least interesting feature of the Autobiography is the glimpse it gives us of Victorian writers. Some of Harriet's literary judgments are curiously inept. They are entirely coloured by her conviction that all literature should inculcate a moral lesson and by her entire lack of imagination. "If Coleridge should be remembered"—we read—"it will be as a warning as much in his philosophical as his moral character." She thinks that his admirers make too much of the "cloud beauty" and the charm and subtlety of his poetry and finds that his eloquence lacks "sound intellectual quality". Alas for the "Ancient Mariner"! But, then, Coleridge drugged himself with opium: and vice and genius, we know, are incompatible. "He amused me not a little," said Harriet; and Coleridge on his part (he had seen the "Series") acknowledged that there were points on which they differed.

She thought but little of Macaulay, the great literary lion of her day—perhaps he roared louder than she did—and in that she is more or less in accord with modern criticism. He was disqualified to appreciate the philosophy of Bacon; he was a plagiarist; inaccurate, and without heart. If he reformed she thought there might possibly be a career in store for him, as he was not without a certain superficial brilliancy. Scott showed a deplorable lack of moral earnestness, and Moore she could not abide. The latter had—like Lockhart—insulted her in a newspaper, so she declined to make his acquaintance. She could not, she said, know people who had "publicly outraged consideration and propriety" and who, incidentally, had treated the "Series" with unbecoming levity! Borrow, too, met with her disapproval; he was a "polyglot gentleman, who appeared before the public as a devout agent of the Bible

Society in foreign parts". She does not mention "The Bible in Spain".

To Dickens she extends a limited and patronizing approbation. She enjoys his peculiar humour—"though many can enjoy it more keenly; indeed, there are many who go beyond me in admiration for his works, and few miss as I do the pure plain daylight in the atmosphere of his scenery. His personages are 'profoundly unreal'," and she wishes he would abstain from writing on different subjects which he does not understand and on which "all true sentiment must be underlain by the sort of knowledge which he has not". Poor Dickens! However, he was her ideal of the "virtuous and happy family man with a glowing heart kept steady by the best domestic influences". Perhaps she changed her mind later on! She contributed some tales on Sanitary subjects to *Household Words*.

Thackeray aroused all that was old-maidish in her virtuous breast. "Vanity Fair" aroused her moral disgust; and *what* a snob he was! "His frittered life and his obedience to the call of the great make him the observed of all observers." Mary Russell Mitford was another author whom she did not like. "Her mind wanted the breadth and her character the depth necessary for genuine achievement in literature." Her conversation charmed at first, but there were defects that sadly impaired its charm. She flattered you to your face and disparaged you to other people: "I never knew her to respond to any act or course of conduct that was morally lofty." Certainly *not* a nice person. Miss Mitford, on her part, damned Harriet with faint praise. "The only things I ever liked were her political economy stories which I used to read, *skipping the political economy*!" . . . "Fifty years hence she will be heard of as one of the curiosities of our age, but she will not be read."

Naturally, she made the acquaintance of Charlotte Brontë. Her account of their first meeting gives one a curious impression of two cats cautiously eyeing each other. Of Mrs. Trollope she said: "I will not dirty my pages with her stories," so let us draw a veil over that deplorable person. Jane Austen met with her approval, probably on account of her unique skill as a storyteller, for she cannot have been capable of appreciating, or even of understanding, the exquisite irony of distinction of that great novelist. It is pleasant to read that Harriet acknowledges to one defect in her literary judgments: It was "an *excessive sympathy*, moral and intellectual", with her author.

Many of the social notabilities of the day flit through her pages. It is amusing to read of the Miss Berrys using the oaths "fashionable a hundred years ago". When the footman told them that Lady —— begged them not to wait for dinner as she was drying her shoes which had got wet between the carriage and the door, the reply was: "Oh, Christ! if she should catch cold!" "My mother heard an exclamation at our door when the carriage door would not open—'My God! I can't get out.' " The Miss Berrys would be quite up to date were they to revisit these glimpses of the moon. Dean Stanley she liked, though he was "the oddest bishop she had ever seen". He refers to her in his letters in rather a non-committal manner, saying that he made her acquaintance on the boat going from Yarmouth to Glasgow. "She behaved very well," he says and attributes it to the fact that she was extremely seasick. Sydney Smith she also liked, preferring his writings to his conversation. His quick wit puzzled her, though she tells an amusing story he invented about Hallam, who loved contradicting everyone. He was ill in bed with influenza, when, hearing the watchman call "Twelve o'clock and a starlight night", he jumped up. "I question that, I question that! Starlight! I see a star, I admit; but I doubt whether that constitutes starlight." An interval of sleep, and he hears the watchman again: "Past two o'clock and a cloudy morning." "I question that, I question that," said he, and, opening up the window notwithstanding his influenza—"Watchman! do you mean to call this a cloudy morning? I see a star, and I question its being past two o'clock," and so on.

Only for Carlyle does Harriet confess an unqualified admiration. He was so moral, and he awakened England to a sense of its sins, infusing into it a sincerity, earnestness, healthfulness and courage previously unknown. Then, too —like Harriet herself—he did not care for fame. "Here, take this," he said to her, holding out a glass of the brandy and water of which he was so fond. "It is worth all the fame in England." And yet there were those who said that he would have been glad of a little more fame.

Men delighted not Harriet: "How vain is man!" she said. She saw Brougham upset by newspaper criticism;

Bulwer, all decked out and perfumed, languishing on a sofa, surrounded by female admirers; Campbell, the poet, quivering with apprehension for fear people should make fun of him; Landseer, holding his cheerfulness at the mercy of great folks' graciousness to him and glancing round, when curled and cravatted he entered a room, to see if he was making a good impression. "There is none that doeth good, no not one," she thought. She herself was not vain, even though she had, as she said, "for a long course of years influenced public affairs to an extent not professed or attempted by many men".

CHAPTER THREE

I T was not, of course, to be expected that the somewhat vague tenets of Unitarianism could continue to satisfy so intellectual a person as Harriet. She replaced it by "Necessarianism"—a doctrine "the truth of which is so irresistible that, when once understood, it is adopted as a matter of course", she tells us. She goes on to say that none but Necessarians understand it, which is unfortunate for those lost in the outer darkness of simpler creeds! Necessarianism killed her belief in Free Will and made her see how irremediable, except by the spread of a true philosophy, are the evils which arise from that monstrous remnant of old superstition—the supposition of a self-determining power independent of laws—in the human will. She could now repose upon "eternal and irreversible laws, working in every department of the universe without any interference from any random will, human or divine", which was a great consolation to her. The New Testament, she found, bore out her theory—the fatalistic element of the Essene doctrine strongly pervading the doctrine and morality of Christ and the apostles. Prayer, as prevailing throughout Christendom, was, she discovered, wholly unauthorized by the New Testament, Christian prayer being precisely the Pharisaic prayer which Christ reprobated. So she changed her method, and, being convinced that everything would happen in its own way irrespective of her prayers, she took for her motto *"Che sara—sara"* and ceased to pray for anything but spiritual benefits for herself. Her views, she felt, were irreconcilable with the notion of the Revelation of a scheme of Salvation; so it was clear that either she or salvation must yield one to the other. Heaven or Harriet, in fact: you could not possibly enjoy both. The subject of Prayer having been thus satisfactorily disposed of, that of Praise remained—fortunately a far less complicated question. God—His functions now sadly curtailed—must, she felt sure, object to being the object of flattery so gross that it would have seemed fulsome even to Queen Victoria; so she ceased to praise Him. Notwithstanding these rather drastic changes in her opinions, she continued a pseudo-acceptance of Christianity.

Harriet was now solidly established as a successful author. The "Series" was finished, and she could place everything she wrote. But she was tired and in bad health, so she decided to take a holiday and go to America. It was a tremendous undertaking in 1834 and meant at least a month's voyage in a sailing vessel. (As a matter of fact, it took her forty-two days to reach New York.) Apart, too, from her need of a holiday, things at Fludyer Street had become very uncomfortable. "My work," she tells us, "afforded an incontestable reason for my being sought and made much of"; but her mother failed to see things that way, and her best friends advised her to leave home for a considerable time "for the welfare of all who lived in that house".

She arrived in the United States at a critical moment;

the country was divided into two camps, Pro- and Anti-Slavery. So burning was the controversy that the captain of the boat did not hesitate to say that if he had known that she was a partisan of either side he should not have hesitated to forbid her to land. He might have known, had he read "Demarara" (one of the "Series"), but that immortal work was little known in the States, and—despite Mr. Wilberforce—public opinion in England was not entirely Abolitionist; indeed, as was subsequently shown during the Civil War, English sympathies were largely with the more cultured and agreeable Southerners. As Harriet went to America ostensibly on a holiday, there was no reason for her to meddle with what did not concern her; but no power on earth could have kept her from meddling. And so, with a refusal entirely feminine to hear anything in favour of those with whom she disagreed, she took sides violently with the "blameless apostles of a Holy Cause", being even foolish enough to speak at an Abolitionist meeting. Worse still, she acknowledged publicly that she saw no harm in marriages between whites and blacks, provided that there was true love on both sides. Americans, she said, freely took negresses as mistresses, and, that being the case, why should they not marry them? Morality demanded it. The racial side of the question never seems to have entered the head of this political economist. What could one do with such a woman? Naturally her want of tact made her very difficult to entertain, for she could never refrain from expressing her opinion on every possible occasion and on every possible question—whether she had studied it or not.

The hospitable Americans behaved admirably to their ungracious guest, doing everything they could for her, however trying the circumstances (and trying they frequently were. In Ohio she was threatened with personal violence if she entered the territory: so her prospective hosts were spared her visit.) She managed to make enemies even in Boston by criticizing American food, though, as she lacked the sense of taste, she might well have left culinary matters alone.

It was a strange country the America of 1834. Travelling was uncomfortable in the extreme. The rough plenty, the violence of the pioneer States, and the crudeness of life in general contrasted curiously with the refined society led by the old Knickerbocker families of New York and the rather finical culture of Boston, where

> "The Lowells talk to the Cabots
> And the Cabots talk only to God,"

—or did in those days! But, all the same, it was hardly so "foreign" to the Englishman as it is now. Harriet did not like the Americans. She found them boastful, conceited and very dishonest. "It is the only instance," said she, "of a nation being inferior to its institutions, and the result will be, I fear, a mournful spectacle to the world. They seem to be relapsing from national manliness into childhood. Their passion for territorial aggrandizement, for gold and for vulgar praise are seen miserably imitated with pious pretensions and fraudulent ingenuity. I fear that the American nation is composed almost entirely of the vast majority who coarsely boast, and the small minority who timidly despair of the republic."

The most exciting of Harriet's American adventures, however, occurred when she came back: she was besieged with publishers demanding a book on America. On the day after her return was announced in the paper they arrived with the milk. Mr. Bentley led the vanguard and was shown into the drawing-room, while Mr. Saunders, of Saunders and Otway, who arrived a moment after and with whom Bentley was on terms of deadly enmity, was taken to another room in order to prevent their meeting and flying at each other's throat. Bentley, blunt and businesslike, offered very high terms for an account of her travels, throwing in as a bribe an offer of £1,000 for a novel. It was not the way to bargain with Harriet. She refused—almost rudely—to consider his proposal. Then came the turn of Mr. Saunders, polite and tactful. *He* suggested £900 and the proceeds of the American sales. She agreed to think it over, and he left her, meeting on the stairs Mr. Colburn. She took an immediate dislike to him. Like Bentley, he could not be made to realize that high-minded Harriet was not actuated by mercenary motives. Her object was to do good; to teach America the error of its ways and to point the moral to England; and if she made money in the process—well, the labourer was worthy of his hire. So Mr. Colburn was dismissed the Presence with a flea in his ear. He left, saying that he should pass the day in a neighbouring café, returning at intervals to flaunt his gold in her face. He had suggested £2,000 for the American book and £1,000 for a novel.

It is difficult to believe that she refused this offer—if indeed it was made—but refuse it she did and accepted that of Saunders and Otley. That authors allowed themselves to be put up to auction and squabbled over by publishers was, she said, a real grief to her. She went to bed disgusted and insulted. (Alas! modern authors are, one fears, less altruistic. "Oh! that Providence would raise up another race of Bentleys and Colburns!" they cry.)

Perhaps Harriet's offended dignity at the suggestion that money was of any interest to her prevented her accepting Mr. Colburn's very handsome offer; perhaps her politically economical mind obliged her to accept the lowest tender. Whichever it was, she signed a contract with the tactful Mr. Saunders. The book, though successful enough, was far from realizing the expectation of its publisher. That anyone managed to get through it is amazing, for it is dull—even for Harriet. One is lost in wonder at her skill in avoiding anything that could possibly be of interest to the general reader. She subsequently wrote a second book, a "Retrospect of Western Travel", which was praised politely by Carlyle and Sydney Smith, who had remained discreetly silent about the first.

Although Harriet had refused to write a novel, the idea had taken root in her mind. Her friends all urged her to write one, so why should she not do so? Writers whom, she felt, were far her inferiors in moral worth and therefore less likely to influence the public for good—

Dickens and Thackeray, for instance—had large circula-
tions. The choice of a subject was difficult. She had read
in the police news an incident which she was sure she
could work up into a novel of the deepest interest, but,
then, she did not care to dwell on the more sordid weaknesses of human nature. Finally she invented a plot of
her own, and the result was—"Deerbrook".

It is an incredibly dull novel, but Harriet disarms criticism by confessing that she was incapable of inventing a
plot. Not that it mattered; she was in good company.
"Dickens cannot make a plot—nor Bulwer—nor Douglas
Jerrold, nor perhaps Thackeray," she notes, while many
really inferior writers, such as Fanny Burney, were able
to imagine excellent ones. And she scorned to imitate
Shakespeare and Walter Scott by borrowing or taking her
story from real life. The scene of "Deerbrook" is laid in
the country and concerns a worthy dissenting family, who
in that happy and unique village are on excellent terms
with the vicar. Perhaps she hoped to rival Jane Austen
who understood so well this eighteenth century country
scene—these virtuous young ladies, their governesses and
their "young gentlemen"—and whose power of story-
telling, gentle irony and delightful style keep us interested
and amused from the first page to the last. But Harriet
was not a Jane Austen, and, truth to tell, "Deerbrook" is
almost unreadable to-day. Not one of her characters ever
lives for a moment. The dialogue is stilted and full of
moral platitudes, and there is not, of course, a single gleam
of humour from beginning to end. There is, however,

one unconsciously funny passage. One of the village ladies of Deerbrook possessed a very violent temper, so violent, indeed, that, having quarrelled with another lady over a pound of butter, she chased her through the village with the reprehensible intention of doing her grievous bodily harm or—even worse—of doing her in! Great was the commotion as, followed by half the population, the ladies pursued their mad career.

We read: "An extraordinary sound became audible, from a distance, above the clatter of plates and the mingling of voices in the summer house.

" 'What in the world is that noise?' asked Margaret.

" 'Only somebody killing a pig!' replied Sydney decidedly.

" 'Do not believe him,' said Mr. Enderby. *'The Deerbrook people have better manners than to kill their pigs in the hearing of ladies on summer afternoons!'* "

Happy Deerbrook!

Did Harriet really receive the startling offers of which she tells us? One can hardly believe it, and yet her nature was thoroughly honest and truthful. Truth and honesty, however, are not incompatible with the wish to impress others with the value of one's wares, be they literary or commercial; so one can only conclude that her colossal vanity caused her to exaggerate. It is significant that when she *did* write the eagerly sought novel it was not published by either of the publishers who made her such brilliant offers on her return from America, *and* it was refused by Murray. The sums paid to popular authors are rarely underestimated—at least by the authors themselves. We read in the "Autobiography" that during Harriet's long career as a writer she earned about ten thousand pounds —little enough for a popular author and not to be compared with the sums earned by many of her contemporaries. One must remember that in those days a popular success had a very large sale, as there were few libraries and people had to buy their books instead of borrowing them.

·   ·   ·   ·   ·

The nineteenth century was getting into its stride. King William had gone the way of all flesh, and Victoria reigned in his stead. Harriet, who had been agreeably surprised at her appearance on her accession, remarks on the change for the worse at the end of a year. "The expression of her face was wholly altered. It had become bold and discontented. Released from the salutary restraints of youth, flattered and pampered by the elated Whigs who kept her to themselves, misled by Lord Melbourne and not yet having found her home, she was not like the same girl that she was before nor the same woman that she has been since. Her mother had gone off the scene, and her husband had not yet come on . . . all her serious mistakes were made while she was in Lord Melbourne's hands." Harriet went to the Coronation, not because she wanted to go, but—admirable woman!— because "it was my clear duty to witness it". She rose at half-past three. She describes the unforgettable scene with that curious lack of imagination which colours—or, rather, makes grey—all her writing. The peeresses did not meet with her approval—"None of the decent differences of dress which, according to middle-class custom, pertain to contrasting periods of life seem to be admissible on these grand Court occasions. Old hags, with their dyed or false hair, drawn to the top of the head to allow the putting on of the coronet, had their necks and arms bare and glittering with diamonds, and those necks and arms were so brown and wrinkled as to make one sick, or dusted over with white powder which was worse than what it disguised." Poor old ladies.

As was only to be expected, the pageantry did not have the same effect on our Harriet as it had on others— "It strengthened my sense of the unreal character of monarchy in England. The contrast between the traditional ascription of power to the sovereign and the actual fact was too strong to be overcome by pageantry, music and the blasphemous religious services of the day. After all was said and sung, the sovereign remained a nominal ruler who could not govern by her own mind and will; who had influence, but no political power; a throne and crown, but with the knowledge of everyone that the virtue had gone out of them. The festival was a highly barbaric one to my eyes. The theological part especially was worthy only of the old Pharaonic times in Egypt. Really it was only by old musical and devotional association that the services could go down with people of any reverence at all. There was such a mixing up of the Queen and the

God, such homage to both, and adulation so like in kind and degree that it made one's blood run cold to consider that this was commended to all as religion. God was represented merely as the King of Kings and Lord of Lords—the lowest of the low views in which the unknown is regarded or described. There is, I believe, no public religious service which is not offensive to thoughtful and reverent persons from its ascription of human faculties, affections, qualities and actions to the assumed First Cause of the universe, but the Jewish or heathen ascription to him of military and aristocratic rank and regal prerogative, side by side with the same ascription to the Queen, was the most coarse and irreverent celebration that I was ever a witness to. The performance of the Messiah, so beautiful and touching as a work of art, is saddening and full of shame when regarded as worship. The promises—all broken; the exultation—all falsified by the event—the prophecies—all discredited by the experience of eighteen hundred years, and the boasts of prevalence, rung out gloriously when Christianity is dying out among the foremost peoples of the earth: all these so beautiful as art or history are very painful when regarded as religions."

There you have Harriet self-revealed, with all her narrowness, with all her want of imagination, of historical perspective, of humanity and of sympathy: she never knew what it was to dream. The symbolism of it all meant nothing to her grey dreary intellect, and she could not lose the opportunity to gird at the religion of others. She was curiously wrong, too, for, say what you will about dogmatic religion, Christ as a living force is as alive to-day as ever. It is strange how stupid very clever people can be. It did not occur to her acute but, at the same time, limited intelligence that the pomp and splendour of a great pageant, the pealing of the organ, the blare of trumpets and the crash of drums, afford a necessary outlet for pent-up emotions that are inherent in humanity. She did not realize that since the dawn of time the majority of mankind, terrified at the utter loneliness of their souls and at the appalling prospect of themselves as the be-all and end-all of existence, have needed, and will continue to need, a religion of some kind "to the last syllable of recorded time". Like the fool, Harriet "had said in her heart, 'there is no God' "; so God must go! It was blasphemous to do Him homage.

She seems to have a special grievance against the Church; "I am," she said, "radically convinced that the intellectual and moral judgment of priests of all persuasions is inferior to that of any other order of men!" Can this dislike have been caused by the advice of the clergyman who at the beginning of her writing career advised her to keep a bottle of Hock in the cupboard and drink a little from day to day when she felt tired until the bottle was empty! If so, one understands it!

Soon after this the strain of a long period of hard work and the difficulties of home life resulted in Harriet's health breaking down completely, and she was an invalid for five years. She spent these years in lodgings in Tynemouth. She was able to continue writing and had the happy idea ot writing a new "Series"—this time "Tales for Children" (of all subjects!). There can hardly have ever existed anyone less capable of understanding and amusing youthful readers. History does not relate if the stories treated of Political Economy in Fairy Land or if they concerned Sanitary subjects, but we may be quite sure that they were of the improving nature so general in those days.

Her illness was diagnosed as a tumour, but that it was entirely nervous trouble is proved by the fact that she was cured by mesmerism. At that time the pathology of the nerves was even less understood than it is now, and treatment by suggestion was not recognized by the medical profession. The case, as may be imagined, made a considerable stir, her doctors being furious. But the controversy brought grist to the mill. She wrote a series of articles on Mesmerism for *The Athenæum*. The Mesmerist was a Mr. Atkinson, whose ideas on religion and science coincided with her own, and with whose help she succeeded in solving every question that perplexes mankind. Her last links with Christianity were now severed. "The Christian superstition," she tells us, "fails to make happy, fails to make good, fails to make wise, and has become as great an obstacle in the way of progress as the prior mythologies which it took the place of nearly two thousand years ago. For three centuries it has been undermined and its overthrow decided"—"In Germany the Christian faith is confessedly extinct, and in France it is not far otherwise." She decided to recognize the "Monstrous Superstition in its true character of a great fact in the history of the race." Naturally her opinions caused her to be looked at rather askance and lost her many friends, but she went her way—as always—regardless of other people.

What was the secret of Harriet's success and influence —for influence she undoubtedly had? She was not a great political writer : her knowledge of most of the questions of the day was, at the best, superficial and was derived from an immense facility for "swotting up" quickly the subject on which she was for the moment concentrating. She had no humour, no charm, and her style was prolix and dull. The truth is—though she would have been the last to admit it—that she was an admirable journalist. To begin with, her methods were those of a journalist. She never corrected, never re-copied, never polished; writing as she wrote letters, "never altering the expression as it came from the brain". Then, too, she had the clever journalist's knack of getting hold of people who really understood the questions of the day and picking their brains. She was, as we have seen, enormously industrious, pushing and quite impervious to snubs. Above all, she was sublimely self-confident and self-righteous—though not self-critical—and genuinely convinced that England looked to her for economic salvation. And so politicians found her very useful. By taking her tactfully at her own valuation—for no flattery was too great for her to swallow—she could be depended on to turn out as many articles as were required on any subject *and* to place them where they would be most useful. Thus Lord Brougham, who had taken her measure exactly, used her to support the new Poor Laws Bill in 1834, and she gave birth to the "Poor Law Tales". Cobden enlisted her untiring pen in aid of his "Corn Laws Bill", and Mr. Bright persuaded her that the state of the Game Laws called for attention. So Harriet—who had probably never seen a pheasant in her life, unless roast— wrote three volumes of entertaining little stories on sport. They did not pay, but the fact that they impressed some young nobleman assured her that they could not but affect "the destination and duration of the Game Laws".

Harriet's real avocation—that of a journalist—was recognized after her retirement to Ambleside, for the *Daily News* engaged her to write two articles a week. Although at so great a distance from London, she was never at a loss for a subject, and it is said that these articles contained her best work—probably because, being less in touch with the political world, she was less didactic and more human. *The Times* never took Harriet at her own valuation, so its writers were "ribald ruffians and scoundrels". They had suggested that she wrote too much. She was twice offered a pension for her services to literature—once by Lord Gray and again in 1873 by Gladstone. She refused, feeling that it would hamper her independence.

CHAPTER FOUR

HARRIET was getting tired of London life, and the novelty of being a literary lion was wearing off. Then, too, people were getting a little tired of her: she had, as *The Times* suggested, written too much and generally in the ungrateful *rôle* of the reformer. There were newer lions; lions that roared "as gently as any sucking dove" or "an t'were any nightingale". Political economy and drainage were all very well in their way, but the nightingale's song was sweeter. You cannot wax *really* enthusiastic over "The Life of a Salmon" or "How to Get Paper"—there were those who thought that Harriet knew too well how to get paper! So she began to feel that it might be as well to seek fresh woods and pastures new. A visit to some friends in the Lake District caused her to fall in love with its charms; she decided to settle at Ambleside and took lodgings for six months while she looked about for a permanent dwelling-place. Her mother, she knew, would be happier living her own life, unvexed by the pangs of jealousy which her inability to share her daughter's social eminence occasioned her. At the end of the six months Harriet was so delighted with Ambleside that she bought a plot of land and built herself a cottage.

The lion of Ambleside was, of course, Wordsworth, with whom she soon became on terms of intimacy. She had no wish to dislodge him from his pedestal; their literary activities ran along different paths. He was a poet, if, indeed, you could call him one, which she doubted. He thoroughly approved of her enterprise, not because such a retreat was an ideal one for a tired worker in bad health, but because "the value of the property will be doubled in ten years". Wordsworth was a tall large-boned clumsy-looking man with a heavy mouth, big nose and glowing eyes. The villagers called him "Horse Face". He and his wife were very kind to Harriet. He had an economical mind and advised her against indiscriminate hospitality. "When you have a visitor," he said, "you must do as we do—you must say: 'If you like to have a cup of tea with us, you are very welcome: but, if you want any meat, you must pay for your board!'" He was generous enough to the poor. "At tea at Rydal Mount," says Harriet, "it was difficult to get cream, because he gave away all the milk to the neighbouring cottagers." She tells us that he was not a man of cheerful temperament or of practical sympathy, and she found his deafness trying. He warned her not to walk too much, saying that his sister had lost both her health and her reason by so doing.

Harriet had no very high opinion of his poetry. She deplored in it "the absence of sound, accurate, weighty thought, and of genuine poetic inspiration"—and he had no philosophy. "As to his poetic genius," she says, "it needs but to open Shelley, Tennyson, *or even poor Keats* (!) to feel at once that few of Wordsworth's pieces are poems." There are, perhaps, few people who will agree with

Harriet that Wordsworth was no poet, but his greatest admirers will admit that his inspiration sometimes failed him. It is difficult to understand how the author of the lines upon Westminster Bridge came to write "The Sailor's Mother" or the touching lyric which runs:

> The beetle loves his unpretending track,
> The snail the house he carries on his back;
> The far-fetched worm with pleasure would disown
> The bed we give him, though of softest down.

Some, says Mr. Wyndham Lewis, have attributed these curious aberrations to Naturalism, others to Neo-Pantheism or the depressing influence of the Lake District. Can it not have been in part due to his friendship with our Harriet? Some of his poems on village life breathe the very spirit of her Poor Law Tales. The mind's eye conjures up a pleasing picture of those winter evenings at Rydal Mount: the old poet shouting "We are Seven" into Harriet's trumpet, and she in her turn obliging with one of her sanitary stories.

Harriet did not lose touch with London. She—like so many of her generation—had a passion for letter-writing, and the letters she wrote to the "gentlemanlike" Mr. Atkinson on philosophy and religion would fill a volume. She also kept up a regular correspondence with Florence Nightingale—the two formidable maiden ladies had much in common. Village life, too, afforded her any number of opportunities for meddling with the affairs of her neighbours. She mesmerized the sick (somewhat against the will of their relations), founded a Workmen's Institute and a Building Society, and gave lectures on the history of England, on sanitary matters and on the evils of drink —this last charmingly illustrated by coloured pictures of a drunkard's stomach, which, she tells us, struck terror into the hearts of the young. She tried to teach the Religion of Humanity to the poor and did not conceal her opinion that if you did not adopt it your mind must be essentially depraved. Farming also came within the scope of her activities. The system in the Lake District she considered bad and wasteful—farmers told her that cows required three acres apiece. She knew *she* could do better and imported a labourer from Norfolk. The experiment seems to have been successful, for she found that even on *her* small plot she could keep "about a cow and a half". Pigs and poultry joined the augmented cow, so the household was well supplied with ham, eggs and milk.

Soon after Harriet's installation at Ambleside she went on a tour of the East—as always—not because she *wanted* to do so, but because it was her duty. Egypt and the Holy Land served merely to convince her how right were her views on religious questions. She had "reached absolute clearness as to the historical nature and moral value of all theology whatever". Faith, she said, had been necessary to men in their early stages; as they advanced they became more reasonable, finally attaining—she hoped—to her own beatific state. She decided to write a book about the East and sketched out her scheme. "There can be but one perfect scheme," she said to a friend, "and this one completely answers to my view." Harriet was not a good traveller—she was far too self-centred. She seems to have taken absolutely no interest in the scenery and art of the foreign countries she visited òr in the customs and idiosyncrasies of their inhabitants. The pleasant human contacts and all the amusing incidents of travel appear to have eluded her entirely. People interested her only *en masse* and in so far as the lives they led under their various governments illustrated her economic theories. It was suggested to her by an Italian whom she met while in Egypt that she should visit Milan to study and write on the Italian question; but really she had no time. Italy must look after itself! Ireland, however, interested her greatly, and she made up her mind that she must certainly turn her attention to solving the problems of that unhappy country.

On her return to Ambleside she occupied herself with translating into English and reducing to two volumes the "Philosophie Positive" of Comte; writing also the book on "Eastern Life" and her "History of the Peace" and sandwiching between these her two weekly articles for the *Daily News*.

But in 1854 she was again taken seriously ill and, when able to travel, went to London to consult a specialist who informed her that her heart was so diseased that she might die at any moment. She put her affairs in order and made her will, leaving her brain to the nation, and, in case, owing to some accident—such as, for instance, her being drowned—the nation were deprived of that priceless heritage, she had a cast of her head made. She then took leave of her friends and returned to Ambleside and—lived on for nearly a quarter of a century.

It was a curious anti-climax and, one imagines, rather a disappointing one. She was tired and ill and not afraid to die, and life held few attractions for her since she could no longer take part in its activities. Then, too, the Christian Mythology, which was now "not only sinking to the horizon but paling in the Dawn of a brighter time", did not—most unaccountably—sink with the rapidity she had foretold, nor did it become appreciably paler. And her expectations had amounted to "absolute assurance"! It was very disconcerting. But on the whole the evening of her life was calm and peaceful. She lived quietly, seeing few friends, writing when she felt able to do so, tending the "cow and a half" and trying to improve her neighbours. Perhaps she discussed her symptoms with that odd old lady, Miss Beevor, who was one of the landmarks of Ambleside and who, when dying, refused to see her doctor as she did not feel well enough.

At last Death, who had tarried so long, remembered Harriet. In 1876 she died, fortified by no rites and in the sure and certain hope of—nothing!

MENDELSSOHN-BARTHOLDY

A FALLEN IDOL

(Felix Mendelssohn-Bartholdy)

CHAPTER ONE

> "Fortune did never favour one
> Fully, without exception."
>   HERRICK.

IF, as Shakespeare tells us, "There's a divinity that shapes our ends", it is certainly a very capricious one and not without a touch of malice, especially towards those on whom it bestows the gift of poetry or music. It creates a Beethoven and strickens him with deafness; a Milton, and takes away his sight. It sends into the world those sweet singers, Schubert and Keats, and inflicts upon them ill-health and every kind of privation and misery, while on others it lavishes everything except the strength of character necessary to enable them to steer their barques safely through the stormy seas of this "troublous life". Only once in a while does it give ungrudgingly with both hands, and it must have waked up in an unusually amiable mood on February 3rd, 1809, the day on which Felix Mendelssohn was born, for all the happy fairies seem to have met round the little boy's cradle, bringing choice gifts and with radiant smiles wishing him "good luck".

The founder of the family, Moses Mendelssohn, arrived in Berlin in 1743 in search of a living. Everything was against him; he was a hunchback and otherwise deformed, and he had to struggle not only against race prejudice and legislation that denied even common justice to the Jew but also with the bigoted orthodoxy and narrow-mindedness of his co-religionists. In spite of this, his intelligence, combined with the tenacity of his race, conquered, and he soon succeeded in placing himself and his family above want. He was a man of wide culture and broad sympathies and made a considerable reputation in Germany as a writer. Of his children, the elder son, Joseph, founded a bank which rapidly grew in importance and is still one of the best-known banking-houses in Berlin. Abraham, the second son—the father of our hero—after a few years in Paris, joined his brother's business and married Leah, the daughter of a rich Jewish merchant named Salamon. They established themselves in Hamburg, in which city Felix and his sister Fanny were born. Owing to the annoyances to which they were subjected by the French army of occupation, they left Hamburg in 1811 and went to live in Berlin. Here everything went well, and with his large fortune and lavish hospitality Abraham soon gained an excellent position. Inspired by the example of his brother-in-law, who had been converted to Protestantism and had taken the name of Bartholdy, from a small property near Berlin owned by the Salamon family, he had his children baptized. Having no particular religious convictions, he wisely considered that it would be unfair to expose them to the social disadvantages of the Jewish Faith, thus—even if baptism was powerless to change their racial characteristics—they were at least spared the reproach of being officially numbered among the Chosen People. He himself was converted a little while after and took the name of Mendelssohn-Bartholdy to distinguish his family from those of his relations who had remained in the tents of Israel.

Felix showed his extraordinary musical talent very early, and he was surrounded by almost ideal conditions for its proper development; for his father had that intense love of culture and the arts—especially music—so often found among Jews. He was master of his household in the old patriarchal sense, but he was a benevolent despot, kind and affectionate, and thought nothing good enough for his children. The best music masters in Berlin, including Zelter, the head of the *Sing-Akademie,* were engaged to teach Felix and his sister Fanny who also had remarkable talent, and he saw to it that not only was their musical training thorough, but that they were given an excellent general education. Their moral training was very strict, and physical exercises were not neglected. Felix was taught gymnastics, swimming, riding and dancing, and throughout his life he loved being in the open air. He was a good-looking amiable boy and devoted to his family with whom his genius soon became a veritable *culte.* When nine years old he made his first public appearance at a concert in Berlin, and from that moment his fame as a *virtuoso* was established. Heine wrote in 1822: "The little Mendelssohn is a second Mozart."

In 1821 a great event occurred in the life of the young musician; Zelter took him to Weimar to present him to Goethe. The author of "Faust" was regarded as being little less than a god by his fellow countrymen: for youth especially he was the object of an almost religious hero worship, and Zelter—a rough, unpolished and rude German of the Stockmar type—shared in it to the fullest extent. Great was the excitement in the Mendelssohn family. "Just fancy," writes his mother, "that the little wretch is to have the good luck of going to Weimar with Zelter for a short time. He wants to show him to Goethe." "Keep your wits about you," said his father, exhorting him to sit properly and behave nicely at dinner, while his sister told him that if when he came home he could not repeat every word which fell from the great man's mouth she would have nothing more to do with him. The child himself was deeply impressed with the importance of the occasion. He described the beautiful arrangements of Goethe's house, the *"Salve"* which greeted him on the door-mat, the statues and the furniture.

"Now, stop and listen, all of you," he wrote to his father. "To-day is Tuesday. On Sunday, the Sun of Weimar—Goethe—arrived. In the morning we went to church, and they gave us half of Handel's 100th Psalm. The organ is large but weak. . . . Two hours afterwards, Professor Zelter came and said: 'Goethe has come—the old gentleman has come!', and in a minute we were down the steps and in Goethe's house. . . . He is kind, but I don't think any of his pictures are like him."

Goethe was far more musical than might have been supposed from his reputation; a reputation perhaps founded on the account of his meeting with Beethoven—possibly he found Beethoven rather loutish and bad-mannered.

Be that as it may, however, they evidently did not take to each other. Goethe's cold indifference after Beethoven had played him his "Moonlight Sonata" drew from that unhappy genius the despairing cry, "But if *you* do not understand my music, who *will* understand it?" He was equally cold and rude to Weber. That he *could* appreciate music is shown in a letter he wrote Zelter after the visit of Felix. "His coming did me a great deal of good, for my feelings about music are unchanged; I hear it with pleasure, interest and reflection. I love its history; for who can understand any subject without thoroughly initiating himself into its origin and progress? It is a great thing that Felix fully recognizes the value of going through its successive stages, and happily his memory is so good as to furnish him with any number of examples of all kinds. From the Bach period downwards he has brought Haydn, Mozart and Gluck to life for me. . . . He took away with him my warmest blessings."

During the visit he was kindness itself to the little boy. He was a very imposing personage and exacted the respect due to his dignity and fame. Even the rough untidy Zelter always wore full dress when dining with him—that is, short black silk breeches, silk stockings, and shoes with big silver buckles—a costume even then long out of fashion and brought out only on very solemn occasions. Goethe gave a party to show Felix off, making him improvise on a theme given by Zelter. He did wonders with it, now making variations on it, now presenting it as a chorale and finally evolving elaborate contrapuntal passages in which, however, he seemed to have quite forgotten Zelter's very commonplace theme! After he had finished, Goethe caressed him, saying, "You won't get off with that: you must play more before we can quite believe in you." So little Felix played him some Bach Fugues, of which Goethe was particularly fond. Then he asked for a Minuet. "Shall I play you the most beautiful one in the whole world?" said the boy, and he played the Minuet from "Don Juan". Goethe was enchanted and put him to all sorts of tests, making him decipher old manuscripts, including an autograph one by Mozart and another by Beethoven, which Felix said looked as if it had been written with a broomstick. Goethe afterwards remarked to Zelter, "Musical prodigies, as far as execution goes, are probably no longer so rare; but what this little man can do in extemporizing and playing at sight borders on the miraculous, and I could not have believed it possible at so early an age." "And yet you heard Mozart when he was seven years old," said Zelter. Goethe agreed but added, "What your pupil already accomplished bears the same relation to Mozart at that time that the cultivated talk of a grown-up person does to the prattle of a child."

The Mendelssohn family had now become one of the most important in Berlin. Owing to their wealth and culture and to the extraordinary *prestige* of Felix, invitations to their house were eagerly sought after, and at their Sunday evening receptions the most notable people in the social and intellectual worlds were to be seen, among others Weber, Gounod, Ingres, Clara Wieck, Rachel and Lablache. It is easy to understand how such an atmosphere must have stimulated the growth of an intelligence so alert and receptive as that of Felix. He had, too, the enormous advantage of being able to direct his compositions and to judge the impression they made on this critical audience, for not only were the best solo singers engaged to perform on these occasions, but also instrumentalists and members of the Dom choir. Although his reputation as a pianist and musical prodigy was exceedingly brilliant, it was not until he was nearly eighteen that he found himself as a composer, when at the end of one of the most beautiful summers ever known—that of 1826—he suddenly arrived at full maturity with his lovely overture to "A Midsummer Night's Dream", a work that he never surpassed and, indeed, rarely equalled. He himself directed its first performance at Stettin where it made an immense sensation.

Among the most frequent guests at the Sunday receptions were Devrient, one of the Court opera singers, and Marx, a distinguished musical amateur with an enthusiastic love of Beethoven's music, the beauties of which he revealed to Felix. Beethoven's sad life had just come to an end in deafness and poverty, and that such glorious works should be practically unknown gave Mendelssohn the idea of starting a movement to nationalize music in Germany and show his fellow-countrymen what a splendid musical heritage they were neglecting. At this period Bach, too, was almost entirely forgotten. Professional musicians admired his compositions for their contrapuntal skill; but their serene beauty and humanity were unguessed at, so much so, that, when in 1828 Mendelssohn and his friends,

Marx and Devrient, persuaded Zelter to give the "St. Matthew Passion", they had the greatest difficulty, not only in collecting and copying the parts, but in finding suitable singers and fighting against prejudice and tradition. All obstacles were overcome, however, and the performance, which had to be repeated, was a triumphant success and marked the first important step in the musical progress of Germany. As Mendelssohn said, it was strange that this great Christian work should have been made known by an opera singer and the son of a Jew! From this time he determined to devote himself to making popular the masterpieces of the past. It must be remembered that in 1829 Germany was only potentially the musical centre it became in the middle of the nineteenth century, largely owing to the efforts of Mendelssohn and his following and of Franz Liszt.

. . . . .

Mendelssohn paid his first visit to England in April 1829. It enchanted him, as did every place where he had a great personal success. In the early nineteenth century England the Puritan tradition was still strong—it is even now very much alive beneath the thin veneer of twentieth century licence—so this German-Lutheran Jew was received with open arms. His reputation for piety and good conduct had preceded him, and, with his wealth, good looks and celebrity—especially as a composer of sacred music—caused him to be almost idolized. He was so different from most of those undesirable foreign musicians; their table manners

were often so odd, and you never knew if they were really
married to the females they brought with them! During
this first visit Mendelssohn played at a Philharmonic Concert
and conducted his "Midsummer Night's Dream" overture.

Henry Phillips, a popular baritone of the day—who, by
the way, sang in "Elijah" when it received its first performance in its completed form in London in 1847—tells
us that Mendelssohn was extremely popular with musicians.
At rehearsals he was invariably tactful and considerate,
praising everyone and—although very easily excited, fidgety
and intensely nervous—never losing his temper. As for the
public, they went wild over him. At one concert, as he
was leaving the platform, an enormously fat Frenchman
rushed at him, took him in his arms and kissed him.
Mendelssohn struggled free and ran, with the Frenchman
in full tilt after him, and some of the orchestra after the
Frenchman whom they finally caught and used rather
roughly. He stormed with rage and cursed them right and
left.

On each of Mendelssohn's subsequent visits he had the
same success, social and musical. Never, says Phillips, was
a celebrity more accessible; he had a smile and a compli-
ment for everybody and everything, and his piercing Jew's
eyes never failed to single out from among a crowd people
to whom he had previously been presented. Curiously
enough he was quite indifferent to dress and on one occasion
arrived at a concert with an enormous hole in his coat.
Young ladies adored him. The sentimental strains of the
"Lieder ohne Worte" tinkled from every piano throughout

the land, and the "War March of the Priests" from "Athalie"—generally arranged as a duet—was the delight of suburban musical evenings. Good Queen Victoria and the music-loving Albert set the final seal on his popularity by honouring him with their unqualified friendship, and he was frequently invited to Buckingham Palace which he describes as "the one really pleasant and thoroughly comfortable English house where one feels *à son aise*!" In a letter to his mother in 1842 he gives a long account of one of his visits there. Prince Albert and Mendelssohn had taken to each other at sight. They were not unlike in appearance, though the Jewish traits were more accentuated in the case of Mendelssohn. Albert had asked him to try his organ before he left England. Victoria joined them, and the royal couple were amiability itself. Victoria even knelt on the floor to pick up some leaves of music which the wind had blown from an open portfolio, and Albert and Mendelssohn helped her. Mendelssohn asked Albert— who began explaining the stops of the organ to him—to play him something "so, as I said, that I might boast about it in Germany." So Albert played a chorale. Like the Duchess in the "Last Minstrel", Mendelssohn

"Liked the harp, he praised its chime,"

saying that Albert's playing would have done credit to any professional. This pleased Victoria, who came and sat beside them. Then it was Mendelssohn's turn; he began a chorus from his "St. Paul". "Before I got to the end of the first verse," he says, "they both joined in the chorus,

and Prince Albert managed the stops for me *so cleverly*. . . .
I was really *quite* enchanted."

Then Victoria asked him if he had written any new
songs, saying she was very fond of singing his published
ones. "You should sing one to him," said Albert. After
the usual protestations that she really couldn't, she decided
she could and said she would try his "Fruhlings-lied" in
B flat, but unfortunately it had been packed up as they were
leaving for Claremont that afternoon. Albert searched
among the music and found a song of Gluck's which she
knew, but in the meantime Mendelssohn had discovered
a set of his own songs and begged her to sing one of them,
which she did, and sang it like a Queen : "Quite charmingly
and in strict time and tune. Only in the line *'Der Prosa
Lasten und Müh'*, where it goes down to D and then comes
up again in semitones, she sang D sharp each time, and
as I gave her the note the first two times, the last time she
sang D where it ought to have been D sharp." The tactful
Mendelssohn was duly delighted with the royal voice and
praised Victoria's breath control. After this he improvised
and finally departed after having begged Her Majesty to
allow him to dedicate his A Minor Symphony to her.
Victoria and Albert did not, apparently, offer to play him
any of the pianoforte duets with which they so often entertained the ladies and gentlemen of the Court.

Before leaving the country he passed a few weeks in
Scotland where the romantic Highland scenery gave him the
inspiration for two of his finest works, the "Hebrides"
overture and the "Scotch" Symphony. The leading theme

of the overture came into his head when he was visiting friends one Sunday, and he had to use all his diplomacy to be allowed to open the piano and play it.

Musical conditions in the England to which Mendelssohn came in 1829, though superficially very different, were—in their essentials—curiously like those prevailing to-day. Then, as now, there existed a small critical public rooted in the best traditions of the past but ready to welcome anything new that seemed to them of real worth. Then, as now, there were those who cried *Ichabod*—"The remembrance of the past", wrote Lord Mount-Edgecumbe, about 1820—"is therefore infinitely more agreeable than the enjoyment of the present, and I derive the highest gratification music can yet afford me from hearing again, or barely recalling to mind, what formerly gave me such unqualified delight." And there was the general public that delighted in sentimental ballads, operatic selections and "Rosebud" waltzes. In these days it derives all the musical culture it is capable of assimilating from Jazz and the sickly retchings of North American Negroes. There is now, of course, a large number of people who crowd the Queen's Hall to listen to Bach or Beethoven, but, in proportion to the population, one doubts if the lovers of good music are any more numerous than they were a hundred years ago.

In the early part of the nineteenth century there was, says Mr. Gardiner in his amusing reminiscences, (1837 to 1853), a great inclination to revive old music. "Madrigals," says he, "are everywhere springing up." Apparently people did not know what they were, so he describes them, saying

that they were best sung sitting round a table, each per-
former having his part *and everyone present being expected
to join in*"! He got up a concert of Tudor music in his
native town, Leicester, but tells us that the Leicestershire
Squires did not appreciate it, though they loved the
exquisitely fresh voices of the boys. Mr. Gardiner did not
care for fugues which he calls "arithmetical music, appealing
more to the head than to the heart". He deplored the bad
manners of Beethoven who did not even acknowledge the
receipt of "a number of his *Adagios*" which he had set to
"sacred words suitable for use in the Anglican Church"!

The most fashionable concerts in Mendelssohn's day
were the famous "Antient Concerts". They were very
aristocratic and very expensive—"applause was rare and
criticism certain". In 1825 the directors were the Archbishop of York, the Duke of Cambridge and Lords Darnley,
Derby and Howe. The chorus included the Children of the
Chapel Royal and the Westminster Abbey Choir-boys. Later
on Prince Albert took a great interest in these concerts.
The programmes consisted of classical music, operatic
selections and sentimental ballads. Sacred music was
generally given at Exeter Hall in the Strand. The huge
orgies of music, such as the ghastly "Handel Festivals",
had not then become popular. The first of them occurred
at the opening of the Great Exhibition of 1851. There were
plenty of first rate singers and instrumentalists to be heard;
among them—Malibran, Grisi, Lablache, Rubini, de Beriot,
Liszt, Thalberg. The titles of the songs then popular reflect
a curiously unsophisticated age—"Farewell to the Moun-

tains", "When Friends look Dark and Cold", "The Old English Gentleman", "Oh, no, We never Mention Her", and the like.

At twenty-four years old Mendelssohn was at the height of his fame as a pianist, and his reputation as a composer was ever-increasing. He was regarded almost as a young god by his fellow-countrymen. In 1833 he was invited to conduct the Lower Rhine Musical Festival at Dusseldorf, then one of the chief musical festivals in Germany. The principal work on that occasion was Handel's "Israel in Egypt", of which he had just discovered the original score. His success was so great that he was offered, and accepted, a three years' contract as director of the Municipal Orchestra. Dusseldorf suited him admirably; he loved the pleasant, easy-going people, and he had perfect liberty to do exactly what he chose. He soon made it a musical centre of the first importance, reviving the works of Allegri, Palestrina and Scarlatti, in addition to those of the great German composers then so neglected. His fame grew daily. In 1834 he was made a member of the Academy of Fine Arts of Berlin and the following year was given the direction of the famous *Gewandhaus* at Leipzig, a rich and solid institution that had been in existence nearly sixty years. At Dusseldorf Mendelssohn had had to organize and create everything; here he found all ready for him: a magnificent choir and a perfect orchestra.

What a delightful town for a musician Leipzig must have been in those days! Every celebrated composer, singer and instrumentalist was to be met there, and the amateur with good credentials could rub shoulders with Mendelssohn, Liszt, Schumann, Joachim and Brahms, and perhaps Wagner and Chopin, not to speak of lesser but still considerable lights—Thalberg, Ernst and David, for instance. Mendelssohn had long wanted to found a Conservatoire of Music there, and some years later, in 1843, he succeeded in overcoming all difficulties, financial and otherwise, and the Conservatoire opened with forty-two pupils; it was the fulfilment of his greatest ambition, and his pet child. It very soon became the most important musical institution in Europe, and its influence on music in Germany and elsewhere was very great. In 1837 Mendelssohn had married Cécile Jeanrenaud, daughter of a former pastor of the French Church at Frankfort. She was a charming girl, pretty and good-tempered, so the life of this darling of the gods was happier than ever.

Perhaps the least satisfactory of all his activities was the part he took in the musical life of Berlin. He had always hated it from an artistic point of view, disliking the cold calculating dry nature of the Prussians. Frederick William the Fourth, who wished to make Berlin the chief centre of all arts, showered honours and decorations on him and in 1840 offered him the post of Principal of the Academy and the direction of the Chapel Royal Concerts. He could not make up his mind to accept. At his father's death in 1835 he had inherited a considerable fortune, and his music brought him in a great deal of money. He consented, however, in the meantime, to direct the religious music given in the Dom and to conduct the Chapel Royal Concerts.

From the first nothing went well; he endured endless annoyance from the political intrigues and the hidebound prejudices of the Court, and he was thoroughly dissatisfied with the orchestra. After the first fifteen concerts he wrote: "I have had fifteen public executions!" Then, too, Liszt had created a *furore* in Berlin, and Felix could never endure playing second fiddle to anyone! He ended his musical connection with the Prussian capital in 1844 and left for London, saying: "The first step out of Berlin is the first step towards happiness." In 1847 he went again to London to conduct the first performance of "Elijah", which was an overwhelming success. It was the final triumph of his brilliant career, however, for at last Dame Fortune began to think that she had done almost enough for our Felix.

His mother, to whom he was devotedly attached, had died in 1842, and her death was a terrible blow. That admirable Jewish quality, love of family and devotion to his own people, was highly developed in him, and now death snapped the remaining link that bound him to the old happy family life by taking away his beloved sister Fanny. Her nature had always been the more robust of the two, and when they were children it was she who encouraged him and spurred him on to fresh efforts. Although very gifted she was content to efface herself entirely and to use her talent and strength of character wholly in his service. He had become accustomed to seek her advice about everything and to rely on her judgment, and he never got over her death. Much as he loved his wife, something deeply racial in him refused to be comforted by her and told him that she had no part in his grief. He became tired out and prematurely old and gave up most of his engagements. On the ninth of October he was taken with a violent chill and high fever, and, although after a short illness he seemed to be getting better, he had a relapse and died on the fourth of November, 1847.

Fortune was kind to him to the end; his fame was at its zenith, and a longer life could have brought only a diminution of his powers and a decrease in his popularity. His was not the genius of a Beethoven or a Wagner ever toiling upwards through sorrow and suffering to reach the distant heights.

.   .   .   .   .   .

Mendelssohn had great personal charm, especially for women, and he loved their society; his love affairs never became serious, however, as he was incapable of passion. He was amiable, generous, fond of dancing and social life, and something of an epicure; but he was also nervous and irritable and in many ways very narrow-minded. He attached a ridiculously exaggerated importance to the minor worries of life, and he was easily offended: for instance, when in 1832 Habeneck refused to give his "Reformation Symphony" at the Paris Conservatoire Concerts, he left France and never returned. The comparative failure of his early and extremely poor opera in Berlin in 1827 so upset him that he did not recover until he had taken a long holiday, and when, after the death of Zelter, the committee of the *Sing-Akademie* would not elect him to the vacant position—partly on

account of his youth and partly because of his Jewish origin
—he never forgot the slight.

He travelled a great deal but always took his prejudices
with him. As we have seen, he loved England; and England
loved him, so all was for the best in the best of all possible
worlds. In spite of the fact that he considered the English
uneducated and with little sense of poetry, he was able to
write from Naples: "That smoky hole London has always
been, and still remains, the place of all others that I like
best." Switzerland, too, enchanted him: "What," he
cried, "is dry Italy beside Switzerland, so fresh and alive!"
He had a curious dislike for France and everything French.
He would not see that Paris after the Revolution was not
the Paris of 1825 whose social brilliance had dazzled him
but with whose musical taste he had been disgusted; and
the genius of Hugo, de Musset, Berlioz and the many other
admirable poets, musicians and writers of that intensely
interesting period left him cold. "How glad I shall be
to return to Germany where there are people who understand what art is and who neither praise nor criticize but
create." This, in the Paris of 1830! In another letter he
airs his antipathy to everything French. "Paris life, in spite
of all its wonderful advantages, has very little attraction for
me. All that one gets from there in the way of composition
is very modern, very piquant, but also very cold and too
seldom natural. Then, everything seems to me *géné* and
exaggerated there, so that I always fancy the musicians
themselves cannot really get any good from their music and
their manner of life. You laugh, perhaps, and see me as

the true Philistine, with a cotton nightcap on my head, and going along with the usual snail's pace of my countrymen." He described Paris as "the grave of every reputation".

That he should be unable to appreciate Italy was only to be expected. He liked Venice, its light, colour and dreamy loveliness, and, above all, Titian's pictures, but he saw in Florence only a dirty medieval town set in a dried-up country and surrounded by bare hills, and the Middle Ages aroused his instinctive hostility. His *bourgeois* soul was unable to realize the aristocratic beauty and reticence of the Tuscan landscape, with its silver-grey olives, its red-brown hills and solemn cypresses standing like sentinels against the deep blue sky. Rome with its museums, pictures and ruins pleased him; he stayed there a long time, going a good deal into society, but he was horrified at the church music, especially as the Jew in him responded to the pomp and ceremony of the Roman Catholic ritual. He writes: "I heard the overture to *Il Barbiere* at the moment of the elevation, and another time an air from *Cendrillon*." At Naples he found the *"Saltarella"* that he used with such effect in his "Italian Symphony". It is difficult to agree with his opinions about Italian singing in general. He compared it to the shouting of drunken men and found it coarse, vulgar and out of tune. This last can hardly be called an Italian defect. He said that Bavarian beer waiters sang better in tune than the greatest Italian *virtuosi*!

As it was with countries, so with people. Mendelssohn never tried to understand any person or any thing that did not at once appeal to his own peculiar temperament, and he took but little interest in the music of other composers of his own day, though always ready to help musicians if it could be done without too much trouble. He wrote to his mother about Berlioz, whose acquaintance he had made in Rome, saying that he had not the least talent, that his music was horrible, and that he was vain, pretentious and beneath contempt from an artistic point of view. Berlioz on his part was quite good-natured about Mendelssohn and admired his talent, but wrote to a friend: "He is a regular porcupine; when one talks about music, one does not know how to take him for fear of giving offence." He was kinder to Liszt and praised his incomparable technique and musical nature, saying that one could not help being fond of him even if one did not agree with his ideas. He was, indeed, far from understanding them, for Liszt, unlike Mendelssohn, who was rooted in the past, was always an inventor and an enthusiastic supporter of anything new that he considered worth while. Chopin was, perhaps, the only contemporary composer for whom he had any real admiration. As he said, they were "Poles apart"; but all the same he recognized his genius both as a composer and as a pianist. When Chopin visited him at Leipzig, he wrote: "Last Sunday evening was very amusing, he (Chopin) asked me to play him my oratorio. Several people had managed to get in without being invited in order to look at him. After the first part of 'St. Paul', he played them his last studies and a new *Concerto*, and then I played the second part of my oratorio. It was exactly as if a Red Indian and a Kaffir

met, and tried to talk to each other." Not a very apt
simile; a Red Indian and a Kaffir at least meet on an equal
plane. How should Mendelssohn, with his sentimental
middle-class mind, understand Chopin's music, its wild
despair and its infinite pity? Even in its gaiety one is always
conscious that "They are not long, the days of wine and
roses", and the sound of the passing bell is never far away:
there is often something strangely suggestive of that dim
borderland between the real and the unreal in its mystery
and terror. And Mendelssohn hated mystery. He called him
"Chopinetto"!

.   .   .   .   .

Mendelssohn's music is characteristic rather than original;
he may almost be called an *electric* with a marked personality. Certain phrases and mannerisms are constantly
reappearing, and there is also an occasional touch of vulgarity, a defect from which no Jewish composer is ever wholly
free; one finds it in Meyerbeer, in Rubinstein and in Saint-
Saens. He considered himself the heir of Bach, Beethoven
and Mozart, but as a matter of fact he was influenced to a
far greater extent by Haydn and Weber, especially the latter.
It is curious that he never developed. He wrote the overture
to "A Midsummer Night's Dream" music in 1826, when he
was a boy of seventeen, and the other numbers in 1840,
fourteen years later, and there is practically no difference
between the work of the boy and that of the man; the style
is identical. The entire work is flawlessly lovely and cannot
but endure. He used the orchestra admirably, but he was

content to follow in the footsteps of his predecessors and to employ each instrument strictly within its own sphere. This he did to such perfection that, like Mozart's, his scoring is often far more effective than that of many composers who search for new effects and orchestral colour. That he could use *colour* when he chose is proved for instance by the warm and lovely combination of the tenor instruments in the second subject of his "Ruy Blas" overture. He had little dramatic sense and never succeeded in writing a successful work for the stage. This he attributed to his being unable to find a suitable libretto, and it was always a great disappointment to him.

He was a remarkably unequal writer. Most of his compositions for the piano, including many of the "Songs without words" that had such a nauseating popularity, are of the super "drawing-room" order; some of them are even "genteel", and the same thing may be said of practically all his songs, part-songs and concerted music for female voices. His best works are undoubtedly the "Italian" and "Scotch" symphonies, the violin *Concerto*, the beautiful *"Variations Sérieuses"* and "Prelude and Fugue in E Minor" for the pianoforte, and the "Hebrides" overture. The *"Concerto"* is an inspired work, fresh, original and intensely musical, and the lovely *Andante* is Mendelssohn at his very best. This type of slow movement is quite his own invention; there are other charming examples of it in his first organ Sonata and in the "Trio in D Minor". The joyous and exhilarating *Finale* of the *Concerto* is really a development of the *Scherzo* form which he found so attractive. His

Scherzi are indeed inimitable; gay, rhythmic and iridescent: in those of the "Scotch Symphony", the "Trio in D Minor" and the "Midsummer Night's Dream" music seems to have taken to herself wings. Of his two Symphonies that have stood the test of time the "Scotch" is by far the best; it is pure music, full of grace and a certain tender melancholy, and sings of the Highland scenery he loved in that slightly vague and dreamy way so characteristic of his style; the *adagio* is very beautiful. One could wish that he had stayed longer in Scotland, for the "Hebrides" overture is also a magnificent work—one of the finest overtures ever written according to Wagner—and it has greater depth and vitality than most of his compositions. The critic of *The Times* wrote of it, "Works such as this are like angels' visits." The "Italian Symphony"; though less fine, is still admirable. The *Adante*, which suggests one of the great church ceremonies that he must often have seen in Rome, is original and not too Mendelssohnian, while the *Finale*, a *Saltarella*, is irresistible in its gaiety and brilliane.

Mendelssohn's Chamber music, though well constructed and melodious, has for the most part little real value, but his exquisite setting of the 42nd Psalm and his *motets*, especially "Hear my Prayer", if not great, have much musical feeling and are likely to survive so long as England produces the lovely treble voices that no other country seems able to equal. It hardly seems that the oratorios "St. Paul" and "Elijah" are destined to achieve immortality. They have neither the sincerity and depth of feeling of Bach's settings of the "Passion"—which were written for the service of the Lutheran Church—not the solidity and grandeur of Handel. Both of them, however, contain magnificent choral writing and music of great lyric beauty, especially "Elijah". There is a sense of drama, to which Mendelssohn rarely attained, in the opening chorus, "Help Lord", with its fine fugue, "The Harvest now is over", and also in the beautiful aria, "Hear ye, Israel". Very moving, too, are the arias "It is enough", with its throbbing accompaniment, and "Then shall the Righteous".

His influence, both in his own country and in England, was very considerable and not altogether good. Even as late as the end of the last century it was said that young musicians suffered from two diseases, measles (Mendelssohn) and scarlet fever (Wagner). His style was unfortunately easy to imitate, and it was enthusiastically adopted by innumerable composers without his genius—among them Horsley, who imitated it so well that it was almost impossible to tell the difference. This resulted in an enormous number of sentimental and emasculate compositions that for many years flooded the concert rooms and churches. Mendelssohn invented the nineteenth century form of oratorio, and the unbounded popularity of "St. Paul", "Elijah" and the "Hymn of Praise" was responsible for the hundreds of unoriginal and conventional oratorios and cantatas written to order for the various musical Festivals during the second half of the last century by composers trained in the German school, whose musical motto was *"Deutschland uber alles"*. On the other hand, his numerous visits to England certainly stimulated an interest in music.

In France he greatly influenced Gounod, and, through him, Massenet and Saint-Saens. His most important work in his own country was the large part he played in popularizing the compositions of the great German musicians and in showing his fellow-countrymen that they possessed a musical literature at least equal to that of any other nation. He helped to create the nineteenth century enthusiasm for music in Germany, that prepared the way for Wagner. But, valuable as was his work, it was certainly no more so than was that of Liszt at Weimar. The wide culture and musical knowledge of Liszt knew no geographical bounds. Pan-Germanism and the intolerant attitude of Germany towards the art of other countries are largely due to Mendelssohn. All the same, he cannot be called to account for the narrow reactionary spirit that manifested itself in Leipzig after his death, chiefly brought about by the Schumanns, Brahms, Joachim and their little mutual admiration society which opposed with tooth and nail every new idea and regarded Wagner as "Antichrist".

After a long period of such adulation and popularity as has been the lot of no other composer, Mendelssohn is suffering a considerable eclipse; it cannot, however, be a total eclipse.

> "So sinks the day-star in the ocean bed
> And yet anon repairs his drooping head."

Even now there are not wanting signs of a revival of interest in his music, especially in France where criticism is a more exact science than it is in England. His genius was undeniable; even Wagner, who was not given to excessive admiration of his brother composers, said: "Mendelssohn is the greatest *specific* musician since Mozart." He was, above all, a Romantic, which makes his failure to appreciate the Romantic movement in Paris all the more puzzling; but he was German to the core, and his romanticism was of an intensely German quality—sentimental, tender and slightly tinged with melancholy. Everything he wrote was melodious, elegant, classic and clear with the clearness of a mountain stream—but mountain streams are shallow, and one constantly feels this lack of depth, even in his best moments. There is none of that struggle to express thoughts and emotions almost too deep for expression that one finds in the later work of Beethoven and, sometimes, in Brahms; there could not be, for Mendelssohn was a creature of facile emotions, and he never tried to write down anything that did not flow easily and naturally from his pen.

He took life with the same ease. It was always for him "A Calm Sea and a Prosperous Voyage". Too prosperous indeed. Rich, successful; happy in his domestic relations and blessed with an extraordinary capacity for enjoyment, he hardly knew sorrow or suffering, nor did he ever have to fight for recognition; so his character, always a little too soft and gentle, was never hardened in the school of life. He himself often said: "I am too happy." Perhaps, had he been less fortunate, he might have risen to greater heights —genius is a plant that needs the shadows as well as the sunshine—but who can tell? The cold waters of adversity, while bracing the strong, often drown the weak, and his character was anything but a strong one. Then, again, he wrote too easily; he had the fatal facility of the talented Jew. Now it is a remarkable fact that the Jewish race, in spite of its great artistic gifts, has never in modern times produced either a poet, painter, writer or composer of the very first rank. Its genius is executive rather than creative and, even so, is distinguished more for its showy qualities than for depth of feeling and interpretation.

It is difficult in these days to be quite fair to the Romantics. Certainly it is impossible to imagine music less likely to appeal to the present restless and neurotic generation, with its slightly bitter outlook and contempt for romance, than that of Mendelssohn. He may be said to have translated into music the average emotions of the majority of his day, and much of what he wrote is already forgotten. There are, however, works of art whose sheer intrinsic beauty sets them high above the changes of fashion and the injuries of time; they are things that "cannot be shaken". Among them I think we may place the "Midsummer Night's Dream" music, the "Hebrides" overture and, perhaps, the "Scotch Symphony". If every modern composer who sneers at Mendelssohn leaves behind him a work as beautiful as any one of these, the world will be the richer.

THE END

BIBLIOGRAPHY

LIFE OF THE PRINCE CONSORT, 5 vols.	Sir Theodore Martin.
EARLY YEARS OF THE PRINCE CONSORT	General Sir Charles Gray.
PRINCE CONSORT . . .	Charlotte M. Yonge.
ALBERT THE GOOD . . .	Hector Bolitho.
QUEEN VICTORIA . . .	Sir Sidney Lee.
QUEEN VICTORIA . . .	Lytton Strachey.
EMINENT VICTORIANS . .	Lytton Strachey.
LEAVES FROM OUR JOURNAL IN THE HIGHLANDS . . .	Queen Victoria.
LIFE OF BARON STOCKMAR, 2 vols.	E. Von Stockmar.
THE GREVILLE MEMOIRS, 1927 EDITION	
THE CREEVEY PAPERS . .	Edited by Sir H. Maxwell.
THE CORRESPONDENCE OF SARAH, LADY LYTTELTON . .	Edited by Mrs. Hugh Wyndham.
REMINISCENCES OF COURT AND DIPLOMATIC LIFE, 2 vols.	Lady Bloomfield.
THE AUTOBIOGRAPHY OF HARRIET MARTINEAU, 3 vols.	
LETTERS OF CHARLES GREVILLE AND HENRY REEVE . .	Edited by A. H. Johnson.
LIFE OF SAMUEL WILBERFORCE	R. G. Wilberforce.
TWELVE GOOD MEN, VOL. II .	J. W. Burgon.
APOLOGIA PRO VITA SUA . .	Cardinal Newman.
SECRET HISTORY OF THE OXFORD MOVEMENT . . .	Walsh.

BARCHESTER TOWERS . . Trollope.

GOETHE AND MENDELSSOHN . M. E. Von Glehn.

MENDELSSOHN . . . de Stoecklin.

FIFTY YEARS AGO . . . Walter Besant.

LIFE OF LORD MELBOURNE . Bertram Newman.

FREETHINKERS OF THE NINE-
TEENTH CENTURY . . . J. E. Courtney.

DICTIONARY OF NATIONAL BIO-
GRAPHY

THE STUFFED OWL . . . W. B. Wyndham Lewis.

MUSICAL RECOLLECTIONS . . H. Phillips, 1864.

MUSIC AND FRIENDS—3 vols.,
1838-1853 . . . W. Gardiner.